Married and Lonely

By

Pastor Garry T. Rodgers

Copyright © 2008 by Pastor Garry T. Rodgers

Married and Lonely
by Pastor Garry T. Rodgers

Printed in the United States of America

ISBN 978-1-60647-822-6

All rights reserved solely by the author. The author guarantees all contents are original and do not infringe upon the legal rights of any other person or work. No part of this book may be reproduced in any form without written permission from the author, except by a reviewer who may quote brief passages in a review to be printed in a newspaper or magazine. The views expressed in this book are not necessarily those of the publisher.

Unless otherwise noted, all scripture quotations are taken from the King James Version of the Bible.

Research on some Scripture and words was found in the various dictionaries.

Traditional Vows from Nelsons Ministers Manual

Photo by Ronald Howell, Newport News VA.

www.xulonpress.com

To my wife Lisa Rodgers whose patience and understanding helped inspire me in writing this book.

ACKNOWLEDGMENTS

I would like to first thank my Lord and Savior Jesus Christ for inspiring me to write this book, and give prayers to everyone who find strength in its contents. I thank my wife, Lisa Rodgers, my son Garry, daughter Sharda', my grandchildren Garry, Princess, and MaRee for their encouragement.

I thank my parents Montgomery and Elizabeth Rodgers, my sisters Sherry, Gail, Angie, Sharlette, and Brother Kelvin, and other members of the Rodgers, Woods, Jones, and Cole family for their unwavering support.

I would like to also give special thanks to my former pastors, Reverend Leotha Rodgers, Bishop John H. Pettiford, Pastor Ron Griffith, Bishop Robert A. Baker, Pastor Renee Williams, and Bishop Joshua Paul Logan for their inspirational commitments.

Special thanks to House of God Worship Center in Hampton VA., for your prayers and support.

Contents

Acknowledgments.. vii
Foreword.. xi
Preface... xiii

Chapter 1
Why Do People Marry?...15

Chapter 2
Marriage Vows..27

Chapter 3
Fairytale Wedding...51

Chapter 4
Need Change Back...57

Chapter 5
Time to Scream..61

Chapter 6
Male Chauvinist..63

Chapter 7
Woman Chauvinist...67

Chapter 8
Holding on Until the End of the Line 73

Chapter 9
Until Death Due Us Part? 77

Chapter 10
The Before and After Marriage 87

Chapter 11
Marriage Vow to Financial Transaction 93

Chapter 12
You Get What You Pay For 97

Chapter 13
Great Expectation 101

Chapter 14
Grow Up 111

Chapter 15
For Husband Exclusive 115

Chapter 16
Single and Free 121

Chapter 17
Open Marriage 125

Chapter 18
Soul Ties 131

Conclusion 137
Food for Thought 147
Marriage Journal 149

FORWARD

The information and research for this book were conducted by married couples from different ethnic origins, races and creeds.

Today's societies are living in a time when everyone has a different opinion about marriage. I have come to the conclusion that what we think about marriage means absolutely nothing compared to what God thinks. Remember the vow that we made to God? Was it a true vow to God or was it just lip service? Marriage is more than a contract; it is an everlasting covenant with God. In biblical times God put the first couple Adam and Eve together. So by that example alone we may assess that a marriage is to be ordained by God; an everlasting investment until death due we part.

We know that God does not make mistakes. The bible say's "And the Lord God said it is not good that the man should be alone; I will make a help meet for him." So when we conduct a study on the subject of Adam being alone, it is critical to focus with a spiritual eye to observe what was occurring during that period; the beginning of creation, man's spiritual assignments, and the replenishment of the earth. God knew that Adam needed a help mate to accomplish such a task.

Adam was married to a woman that he didn't select, nevertheless God knew what was best for him. That's why Adam said, "this is now bone of my bones, and flesh of my flesh: she shall be called woman, because she was taken out of man". Adam never imagined that his wife Eve would one day influence him to make a critical decision that would have long lasting affects between man and his Creator.

Author

PREFACE

Devotees may wonder how a person of twenty years of marriage could write a book concerning marriage and loneliness. However, through God's guidance all things are possible.

There is no perfect marriage. What a person puts in is what is usually harvested. People are different in some ways which doesn't always represent a positive out come. Differences often generate conflicts of interest, which is common in many relationships. However, if baptized in the name of Jesus, filled with the Holy Ghost, with the evidence of speaking in tongues, there are no mountains, or any form of adversities that a sanctified Christian can not triumph over.

Before a reader or an audience criticize this book, let them first sit back, relax, and enjoy the ride. Remembering to put your seat belt on before getting a ticket!

It is often asked what do the words "Married and lonely" mean? Well, married means to join as husband and wife; a close union within the confinements of the laws of God. The word lonely is defined as being without company or lonesome; a complexity of being out of touch!

Clearly the words mean different things. Actually they are totally the opposite in definition. Marriage talks about the concept of personal spiritual commitments, while loneliness confers with the state of alienation.

The Scriptures focus a great deal about marriage, and its principal code of honor. God is the same today as yesterdays never reverse His code of matrimony (Mal. 3:6; Matt. 19:6; 24:35).

PRAYER

"Father in the precious name of Jesus, I thank you for being the one and true living God in our life. I pray that you have your way in every marriage ceremony that stands before your presence. Forgive that husband and wife who has allowed the devil to have free reign in their marriage. I come against that spirit of loneliness, hurt, bitterness, divorce, abuse, and selfishness. Lord we need Your Spirit to have its way in this relationship. Put the freshness back into this romance. And Lord touch that spouse who could not take the pressure in their union and the outcome ended up tragic or fatal. Let that man or woman know that there is life left in every dry situation, and nothing in life happens without your approval. We thank you for your grace and your mercy. And Lord forgive the couple whose marriage vows that were not carried out in your name. Against you and you only have we sinned. So forgive the couple who has stepped out of your will and committed adultery and infidelity; not knowing how much damage they were causing. In Jesus name amen

Chapter 1

WHY DO PEOPLE MARRY?

Asking the question of why people marry is similar to why people spend thousand of dollars within a day, without having the slightest idea of what they're getting into. The first thing a person should ask before walking down an aisle is what are they getting themselves into, and how well do they know their selected mate. If a person can't answer these critical questions before they take marital vows, and feel quite secure as to why they're getting married, it may be one the biggest rides of their life! However, if a person feels mistrustful about marring before even enquiring into the trials of marriage, then their skepticism may be their greatest warnings.

These are just a few reasons why people get married:

- Love
- Finance
- Companionship
- Sex
- Obligation
- Time clock / Biological clock
- Parental pressure
- Children
- Friendship

- Physical attraction
- Talent
- Revenge
- Security
- Pregnancy
- Titles/Positions

People marry for various reasons. To get even or just out of pure spite! In today's Christian churches there are a lot of couples getting married, just because they believe it's the "in thing" and that being single is no more an acceptable state. Another factor is the ratio of twelve waiting women to one man, which compels many females to accept the first guy who asks for their hand in marriage. Last, but not least, some individuals marry with the belief that a marriage will solve all of their problems.

The bible says "He that findeth a wife findeth a good thing". So if a women or young lady is not asked for her hand in marriage, does it means she's no good, not worth any thing, or just cursed? Absolutely not! It just means that it is not her time, which gives her more space to analyze greater avenues, before walking into a situation she never prepared for. Now that's wisdom!

It is obvious that people who do not obey the word of God avoids more pressure than those who do. Their integrity level is not as high; as they appear to do a lot of things to relieve themselves of life's pressures and pleasures.

A person does what they feel is natural when they live outside the rules of God. Ha, boy meet girl, boy likes girl! For example: men love cars, and before favoring a car, they will test drive it before making a purchase. While observing they will likely move on to the next car, until he finds the right one. Such behavior can be compared between a couple's relationships; a relationship that is tested year by year only to find that it never works.

In a metaphoric practical since, some items make it off the manufactory assembly line, just to go through a recall because of malfunctions, which causes serious body harm, or death. That is how some marriages work today; looking good, running good but needs to be recalled because of a life or death danger it may impose.

Being lonely in a marriage in many ways can be more than just a mental state of loneliness. It can also be very brutal or physical; neither of which is good for a marriage.

Marriages comes under attack from the very second the vows are read, and every day after. Couples shouldn't look at someone else marriage and say that's how I want mine to be, based on an assumption that marriages are made in heaven. Couples must be cautious to avoid judging or comparing outside marriages to their own.

Many couples are still trying to figure out where they went wrong, or what happened in their relationship. The questions that people are frightened to inquire upon while dating. There are some couples who didn't favor certain things about their mate before getting married, but in their own conviction thought they could personally change their mate. How many of the below questions couples asked their mates before matrimony? Let's face it, by asking certain questions before making one's vow could have saved many marriages!

Communication:

- Do you talk when you are upset?
- Are you a selfish person?
- Do you want children? If so, how many?
- Are you married?
- Have you ever been married?
- How many times have you been married?
- How many children do you have? Do you support them?
- Have you ever been abusive- verbally, mentally, or physically?
- What are your goals in life?
- Do you have a criminal record?
- What's your educational back ground?
- What are your views on marriage?
- How's your sanitation and cleanness, at home?
- Do you love and respect your father, mother, sister and brother?

Health:

- Are you able to have children?
- Do you have any mental condition?
- What's the health history of your family?
- How's your health at the present time?
- Have you ever been tested for AIDS before marriage?
- Can I research your medical record?
- What surgery have you had?
- Paranoia?
- What venereal diseases have you contracted?
- Manic depression?
- Can I get a record from the city health clinic on you?
- How many abortions have you had?
- Eating disorder?
- Bipolar disorder?
- Do you have any known transmittal disease?

Sexually:

- Any same sex relationships?
- Do you practice masturbation?
- How often do you like to have sex?
- Can you perform sexually?
- Are you a giver or a taker?
- Have you ever been raped?
- Suffered molestation?
- Are you into any bondage sex?
- Have you ever had sex with an animal?
- How many partners have you had?
- How do you feel about sexual dissatisfaction?
- Are you affectionate?
- Are you into anal sex?
- Are you into oral sex?
- Are you into orgies?
- Have you ever had sex with a minor?

Habit:

- Do you gamble?
- Have you done drugs and how often?
- Have you ever been addicted to drugs?
- Have you sold drugs and how much?
- Do you smoke?
- Do you drink and how much?
- Do you a lie?
- Have you ever gotten into pornography?
- Shopping?
- Have you ever had any internet affairs?

Financial:

- What's your work history?
- Do you work?
- How long have you ever held a real job?
- Student loans?
- Do you have any out standing bills?
- Do you pay bills on time?
- How many times have you been fired from a company?
- Child support?
- How many hours a week do you work?
- Spending addiction?
- How many bankruptcies have you had?
- Has your job ever been a reason for a break up in your relationship?
- Credit report?
- Any Garnishment?
- How many jobs have you quite?

Married secrets:

- Adultery
- Internet affairs
- Married to someone else

- Child not his
- On the down low
- Incest
- Murder
- Cross dresser
- Transvestite
- Pedophile
- Rapist
- Compulsive liar
- Homosexual
- Lesbian
- Robbery

Education:

- What is your view on education?
- Did you graduate from high school?
- Did you attend any special education class?
- What was your grade point average?
- What degrees do you have?
- Were you a high school drop out?
- Do you have any college courses?

Religion:

- Do you believe in God?
- Do you love Jesus?
- Do you believe Jesus is Lord?
- Do you have the Holy Ghost according to the Scripture?
- Do you believe that the baptism is a part of Salvation?
- Have you been baptized in Jesus name?
- Do you believe in women preachers?
- Do you study or read the bible?
- Are you a prayer warrior?
- How often do you attend church?
- What is your religious point of view on divorce?
- Do you believe in giving tithes and offering?

Parenthood:

- Do you have children?
- Do you love children?
- Will you love my children?
- Do you want children?
- What is your input on adoption?
- Do you use birth control?
- How do you discipline children?
- Do you believe in correcting children?
- Any abortions?
- Do you believe in abortions?

Signs of a troubled marriage:

- No respect for each other
- Avoiding each other
- Coldness
- Fighting
- Lost trust
- Sleeping in separate rooms
- Spouse asking for a divorce
- Hiding cell phone and phone bills
- Living in separate homes
- Want a marriage separation
- Infidelity/Adultery
- Working seven days a week
- Do not want to change
- Disappearing at different hours
- Stop wearing wedding ring
- No concern for spouse
- You no longer have fun together
- Staying away from home
- Down grading one another at home and in public
- Lost love
- Little or no communication
- Always talking about old relationship

- Secret text messages and received calls
- Not answering the cell phone at odd hours.
- Excessive spending
- In love with someone else
- Not spending time with spouse
- Feels resentment
- Your children begin to acts out from stress
- Clothes smell different
- Living under the microscope
- Email affairs
- Making love to yourself (having sex to please yourself and not your spouse)
- Secret marks on the body
- Unequally yoked

Here are some Scriptures from the bible that discuss the importance of God's plan for marriage. In marriage we need all the help we can get. Whenever couples go into marriage not wanting help from God, that couple will be headed down the road of destruction. I'm speaking from experience. This is a true testimony; without God in my marriage it would not be a marriage at all. It will only be a living arrangement between two adults trying to make something work on their own...

Marriage is described as:

- Blessed by God for having children................... Gen. 1:27-28
- Instituted by God.. Gen. 2:18-24
- Means of sexual love..Prov. 5:15-19
- Honored in all..Heb. 13:4
- Permanent bond...Matt. 19:6
- Intimate bond ....Matt. 19:5
- Dissolved by death.. Rom. 7:2-3
- Centered in love and obedience Eph.5:21-33
- Worthy of Jesus presence ....John. 2:1-11
- Love flows...1 Cor. 13:5
- Trouble 1Cor.7:27-28
- One flesh ....Mk 10:8-9

The book of 1Corinthians used very often for married couples today. It is an example to show us what some people may be going through or have gone through in their marriage at one point or another. So many people read this part of the bible but do not study what Paul was really saying about marriage. Although Paul was not married in his life time, he had a lot of wisdom on the subject. So take a look at this book and see how much a single man (Paul) can teach us about being married. After Studying the book of Corinthians, we might see some reasons why we get married.

Paul is talking about:

Being single
Staying single
Warring with your hormones
Marriage
Fornication
Husband and wife with holding sex
Speaking out of flesh
Divorce
Saving your marriage

1 Corinthians 7

¹Now concerning the things whereof ye wrote unto me: It is good for a man not to touch a woman.

²Nevertheless, to avoid fornication, let every man have his own wife, and let every woman have her own husband.

Point: marriage alone will never stop a person from fornication. What stops a man or woman is the love of Jesus Christ

³Let the husband render unto the wife due benevolence: and likewise also the wife unto the husband.

Point: when couples get married they are giving their body to their spouse for pleasure.

⁴The wife hath not power of her own body, but the husband: and likewise also the husband hath not power of his own body, but the wife.

Point: Your spouse has power over your body, so you really need to know what you are getting into before you say I do.

⁵Defraud ye not one the other, except it be with consent for a time, that ye may give yourselves to fasting and prayer; and come together again, that Satan tempt you not for your incontinency.

Point: Defraud is a strong word, do not let yourself be the reason your spouse has gone outside the marriage.

⁶But I speak this by permission, and not of commandment.
⁷For I would that all men were even as I myself. But every man hath his proper gift of God, one after this manner, and another after that.
⁸I say therefore to the unmarried and widows, it is good for them if they abide even as I.

Point: Paul is saying , being single is not the end of the world.

⁹But if they cannot contain, let them marry: for it is better to marry than to burn.

Point: Now if you just can't contain yourself, please get married, before you get yourself into trouble.

¹⁰And unto the married I command, yet not I, but the Lord, Let not the wife depart from her husband:

Point: Divorce is not from God. Yes it is a popular thing right now but God is still not in it. On the other hand if your spouse divorces you. It is nothing you can do about that. You can not make a person love you.

Married and Lonely

¹¹But and if she depart, let her remain unmarried or be reconciled to her husband: and let not the husband put away his wife.

¹²But to the rest speak I, not the Lord: If any brother hath a wife that believeth not, and she be pleased to dwell with him, let him not put her away.

¹³And the woman which hath an husband that believeth not, and if he be pleased to dwell with her, let her not leave him.

¹⁴For the unbelieving husband is sanctified by the wife, and the unbelieving wife is sanctified by the husband: else were your children unclean; but now are they holy.

¹⁵But if the unbelieving depart, let him depart. A brother or a sister is not under bondage in such cases: but God hath called us to peace.

¹⁶For what knowest thou, O wife, whether thou shalt save thy husband? or how knowest thou, O man, whether thou shalt save thy wife?

¹⁷But as God hath distributed to every man, as the Lord hath called every one, so let him walk. And so ordain I in all churches

Chapter 2
=========

MARRIAGE VOWS
(The break down)

Marriage vows are just as important today as many years ago. The vows below are the old traditional ones that have been used in millions of marriages throughout the centuries. There are so many different marriage vows out there; until it is believed that many are individually invented.

Vows in marriages are nothing but a contract between God and man, and at times need no witnesses to confirm a union. Marriage traditional oaths exercised by wedding officiates, are repeated by the groom, and then in turn by the bride.

The meaning of the below vows are a break down of God's requirement. To recite the below vow is a refresher to one's past and present commitments.

("I, Groom/Bride first name, Take thee, Groom/Bride first name, To be my *(wife/husband)*; To have and to hold from this day forward, for better for worse, for richer for poorer, in sickness and in health, To love and to cherish, til death us do part, according to God holy ordinance; and there to do I give thee my pledge.)

A BREAK DOWN OF EVERY WORD YOU SAID IN YOUR VOWS

vow[1]   (vou)
n.

1. An earnest promise to perform a specified act or behave in a certain manner, especially a solemn promise to live and act in accordance with the rules of a religious order: *take the vows of a nun.*
2. A declaration or assertion.

v. **vowed, vowing, vows**
v. tr.

1. To promise solemnly; pledge. See Synonyms at promise.
2. To make a pledge or threat to undertake: *vowing revenge on their persecutors.*

v. intr.
　　To make a vow; promise.

I[1]   (ī)
Point: when you used the word "I", you are making it personal to God and your spouse, that's why you stated your name. To make sure you are in a right state of mind.
pron.

Used to refer to oneself as speaker or writer.
n. pl. **I's**

The self; the ego.

Married and Lonely

take (tāk)

(Garry) Now you are about to take possession of something for a life time. You are getting ready to seize someone you have been waiting for.

v. **took,** (to͞ok) **taken,** (tā'kən) **taking, takes**
v. tr.

1. To get into one's possession by force, skill, or artifice, especially:

    a. To capture physically; seize: take an fierce enemy fort.
    b. To seize with authority; confiscate.
    c. To kill, snare, or trap (fish or game, for example).

You *pron.*

1. Used here to refer to the one or ones being addressed: *I'll lend you the book. You shouldn't work so hard.* See Regional Note at you-all. See Regional Note at you-uns.
2. Used to refer to an indefinitely specified person; one: *You can't win them all.*
3. <u>Nonstandard.</u> Used reflexively as the indirect object of a verb: *You might want to get you another pair of shoes*

to (to͞o; tə *when unstressed*)
prep.

1.
    a. In a direction toward so as to reach: *went to the city.*
    b. Towards: *turned to me.*

2.
    a. Reaching as far as: *The ocean water was clear all the way to the bottom.*
    b. To the extent or degree of: *loved him to dis- stract him.*

c. With the resultant condition of: *nursed her back to health.*

be (bē)
v. First and third person singular past indicative **was,** *(wŭz, wŏz; wəz when unstressed)second person singular and plural and first and third person plural past indicative* **were,** *(wûr)past subjunctive participle* **been,** *(bĭn)present participle* **being,** *(bē'ĭng)first person singular present indicative* **am,** *(ăm)second person singular and plural and first and third person plural present indicative* **are,** *(är)third person singular present indicative* **is,** *(ĭz)present subjunctive* **be**
v. intr.

1. To exist in actuality; have life or reality: *I think, therefore I am.*
2.
   a. To occupy a specified position: *The food is on the table.*
   b. To remain in a certain state or situation undisturbed, untouched, or unmolested: *Let the children be.*
3. To take place; occur: *The test was yesterday.*
4. To go or come: *Have ever been to Italy? Have you been home recently?*
5. Used as a copula in such senses as:
   a. To equal in identity: *"To be a Christian was to be a Roman"* (James Bryce).
   b. To have a specified significance: *A is excellent, C is passing. Let N be the unknown quantity.*
   c. To belong to a specified class or group: *The human being is a primate.*
   d. To have or show a specified quality or characteristic: *She is witty. All humans are mortal.*
   e. To seem to consist or be made of: *The yard is all snow. He is all bluff and no bite.*
6. To belong; befall: *Peace be unto you. Woe is me.*

my (mī).

(Garry) my means, you become my possession, I am your's and you are mine. And we also have papers to prove it.

adj. The possessive form of I¹.

1. Used as a modifier before a noun: *my boots; my accomplishments.*
2. Used preceding various forms of polite, affectionate, or familiar address: *My friend, you are so right.*
3. Used in various interjected phrases: *My word! My goodness!*

wife (wīf).

n. pl. **wives** (wīvz)
A woman joined to a man in marriage; a female spouse.

husband (hŭz'bənd) *n.*

1. A man joined to a woman in marriage; a male spouse.
2. <u>Chiefly British.</u> A manager or steward, as of a house- hold.
3. <u>Archaic.</u> A prudent, thrifty manager.

have (hăv)

(Garry) to have is everything you own becomes mine and every- thing I have becomes yours. And everything means everything.

v. **had,** (hăd) **having, has** (hăz)
v. tr.

1.
    a. To be in possession of: *already had a car.*
    b. To possess as a characteristic, quality, or function: *has a beard; had a great deal of energy.*
    c. To possess or contain as a constituent part: *a car that has air bags.*

and (ənd, ən; ănd *when stressed*)
conj.

1. Together with or along with; in addition to; as well as. Used to connect words, phrases, or clauses that the same grammatical function in a construction.
2. Added to; plus: *Two and two makes four.*
3. Used to indicate result: *Give the boy a chance, and he might surprise you.*
4. *Informal.* To Used between finite verbs, such as *go, come, try, write,* or *see: try and find it; come and see.* See Usage Note at try.
5. *Archaic.* If *and it pleases you.*

hold[1] (hōld)

(Garry) to hold is when we are so tight and entangle that we would not let each other go under any circumstance.

v. **held,** (hĕld) **holding, holds**
v. tr.

1.
    a. To have and keep in one's grasp: *held the reins tightly.*
    b. To aim or direct; point: *held a hose on the fire.*
    c. To keep from falling or moving; support: *a nail too small to hold the mirror; hold the horse steady; papers that were held together with staples.*
    d. To sustain the pressure of: *The old bridge can't hold much weight.*

from (frŭm, frŏm; frəm *when unstressed*)
prep.

1.
    a. Used to indicate a specified place or time as a starting point: *walked home from the station;*

from six o'clock on. See Usage Note at http://dictionary.reference.com/search?q=escape See Usage Note at whence.

    b. Used to indicate a specified point as the first of two limits: *from grades four to six.*

this (*th*ĭs)
pron. pl. **these** (*th*ēz)

1.
    a. Used to refer to the person or thing present, nearby, or just mentioned: *This is my cat. These are my tools.*
    b. Used to refer to what is about to be said: *Now don't laugh when you hear this.*
    c. Used to refer to the present event, action, or time: *said he'd be back before this.*

day (dā)

(Garry) this means you gave God a day to remember, it was like a birthday and does not expire until death.

1. The period of light between dawn and nightfall; the interval from sunrise to sunset.
2.
    a. The 24-hour period during which the earth completes one rotation on its axis.
    b. The period during which a celestial body makes a similar rotation.
3. *Abbr.* **D** One of the numbered 24-hour periods into which a week, month, or year is divided.
4. The portion of a 24-hour period that is devoted to work, school, or business: *an eight-hour day; a sale that lasted for three days.*
5. A 24-hour period or a portion of it that is reserved for a certain activity: *a day of rest.*

6.
   a. A specific, characteristic period in one's lifetime: *In Grandmother's day, skirts were long.*
   b. A period of opportunity or prominence: *Every defendant is entitled to a day in court. That child will have her day.*
7. A period of time in history; an era: *We studied the tactics used in Napoleon's day. The day of computer science is well upon us.*
8. **Days** Period of life or activity: *The sick cat's days will soon be over.*

forward (fôr'wərd)

(Garry) you told God that this relationship will continue to move forward, no matter what the circumstance.

1.
   a. At, near, or belonging to the front or fore part; the forward section of the aircraft.
   b. Located ahead or in advance: kept her eye on the forward horizon.
2.
   a. Going, tending, or moving toward a position in front: a forward plunge down a flight of stairs.
   b. *Sports.* Advancing toward an opponent's goal.
   c. Moving in a prescribed direction or order for normal use: forward rolling of the cassette tape

for (fôr; fər *when unstressed*)
prep.

1. Used to indicate the object, aim, or purpose of an action or activity: *trained for the ministry; put the house up for sale; plans to run for senator.*
   a. Used to indicate a destination: *headed off for town.*
   b. Used to indicate the object of a desire, intention, or perception: *had a nose for news; eager for success.*

2. Used to indicate the object of a desire, intention, or per-perception: *had a nose for news; eager for success.*
3.
   a. Used to indicate the recipient or beneficiary of an action: *prepared lunch for us.*
   b. On behalf of: *spoke for all the members.*
   c. In favor of: *Were they for or against the proposal?*
   d. In place of: *a substitute for eggs.*

better[1]

(Garry) This is the part we love, the better. The better is with your degrees, education, promotion, slim body, beautiful hair, pretty skin, and so on.

adj. Comparative of good.
1. Greater in excellence or higher in quality.
2. More useful, suitable, or desirable: *found a better way to go; a suit with a better fit than that one.*
3. More highly skilled or adept: *I am better at math than English.*
4. Greater or larger: *argued for the better part of an hour.*
5. More advantageous or favorable; improved: *a better chance of success.*
6. Healthier or more fit than before: *The patient is better today.*

worse (wûrs)

(Garry) worse is the negative side, weight gain, lost of romance, lost of communication, bad sex, boring, can not cook, can't get along.

adj. Comparative of bad[1]., ill.
1. More inferior, as in quality, condition, or effect.
2. More severe or unfavorable.
3. Being further from a standard; less desirable or satisfactory.
4. Being in poorer health; more ill.

rich (ℝĭch)

(Garry) Rich is when you lack no material thing and everything is right at your hand. Do not have to beg for anything. Need no assistance.

adj. **richer, richest**

1. Possessing great material wealth: "Now that he was rich he was not thought ignorant any more, but simply eccentric" (Mavis Gallant).
2. Having great worth or value: *a rich harvest of grain.*
3. Magnificent; sumptuous: *a rich brocade.*
4.
    a. Having an abundant supply: *rich in ideas.*
    b. Abounding, especially in natural resources: *rich land.*
5. Meaningful and significant: " a rich sense of the transaction between writer and reader" (William Zinsser).
6. Very productive and therefore financially profitable: *rich seams of coal.*
7.
    a. Containing a large amount of choice ingredients, such as butter, sugar, or eggs, and therefore unusually heavy or sweet: *a rich dessert.*
    b. Having or exuding a strong or pungent aroma: "Texas air is so rich you can nourish off it like it was food" (Edna Ferber).
8.
    a. Pleasantly full and mellow: *a rich tenor voice.*
    b. Warm and strong in color: *a rich brown velvet.*
9. Containing a large proportion of fuel to air: *a rich gas mixture.*

Poorer (po͝or)

(Garry) Poorer is what we do not want in a marriage. Poorer will test any marriage. Poorer means we are not in the suburbs', we can not buy that new car every four years, and the trailer park or projects do not look bad after all.

adj. **poorer, poorest**

10. Having little or no wealth and few or no possessions.
11. Lacking in a specified resource or quality: *an area poor in timber and coal; a diet poor in calcium.*
12. Not adequate in quality; inferior: *a poor performance.*
13.
    a. Lacking in value; insufficient: *poor wages.*
    b. Lacking in quantity: *poor attendance.*
14. Lacking fertility: *poor soil.*
15. Undernourished; lean.
16. Humble: *a poor spirit.*
17. Eliciting or deserving pity; pitiable: *couldn't rescue the poor fellow.*
18. *rmal.* Highly amusing.

in¹ (ĭn)
prep.

1.
    a. Within the limits, bounds, or area of: *was hit in the face; born in the spring; a chair in the garden.*
    b. From the outside to a point within; into: *threw the letter in the wastebasket.*
2. To or at a situation or condition of: *was split in two; in debt; a woman in love.*
3.
    a. Having the activity, occupation, or function of: *a life in politics; the officer in command.*
    b. During the act or process of: *tripped in racing for the bus.*

4.
- a. With the arrangement or order of: *fabric that fell in luxuriant folds; arranged to purchase the car in equal payments.*
- b. After the style or form of: *a poem in iambi pen- tameter.*

5. With the characteristic, attribute, or property of: *a tall man in an overcoat.*

6.
- a. By means of: *paid in cash.*
- b. Made with or through the medium of: *a statue in bronze; a note written in German.*

7. With the aim or purpose of: *followed in pursuit.*
8. With reference to: *six inches in depth; has faith in your judgment.*
9. Used to indicate the second and larger term of a ratio or proportion: *saved only one in ten.*

sickness (sĭkns)
n.

1. The condition of being sick; illness.
2. A disease in the body
3. A disease; a malady.
4. A defective or unsound condition.

sickness (sĭk'nĭs)
n.

1. The condition of being sick; illness.
2. A disease or an illness.

Main Entry: **sickness**
Pronunciation: 'sik-n&s
Function: *noun*

1. The condition of being ill (ill health)
2. A specific disease

3. nausea

(Garry) this means one day that old body is going to have some problems. With sickness, the body might not regain its normal appearance after medication. Can a person love another in such state without wanting someone new?

health (hĕlth)
n.

1. The overall condition of an organism at a given time.
2. Soundness, especially of body or mind; freedom from disease or abnormality.
3. A condition of optimal well-being: *concerned about the ecological health of the area.*
4. A wish for someone's good health, often expressed as a toast.

love (lŭv)
n.

1. A deep, tender, ineffable feeling of affection and solicitude toward a person, such as that arising from kinship, recognition of attractive qualities, or a sense of underlying oneness.
2. A feeling of intense desire and attraction toward a person with whom one is disposed to make a pair; the emotion of sex and romance.
3.
    a. Sexual passion.
    b. Sexual intercourse
    c. A love affair
4. An intense emotional attachment, as for a pet or treasured object.
5. A person who is the object of deep or intense affection or attraction; beloved. Often used as a term of endearment.
6. An expression of one's affection: *Send him my love.*

7.
   a. A strong predilection or enthusiasm: *a love of language.*
   b. The object of such an enthusiasm: *The out-doors is her greatest love.*
8. **Love** *Mythology.* Eros or Cupid.
9. Often **Love** *Christianity.* Charity.
10. *Sports.* A zero score in tennis.

cherish (chĕr'ĭsh)
tr.v. **cherished, cherishing, cherishes**

1. To treat with affection and tenderness; hold dear: *cherish one's family; fine rugs that are cherished by their*
2. To keep fondly in mind; entertain: *cherish a memory.* See Synonyms at appreciate.

till² (tĭl)
prep.
Until.

death (dĕth)

(Garry) Death is the appropriate and only time in God's eyes end marriage.

1. The act of dying; termination of life.
2. The state of being dead.
3. The cause of dying: *Drugs were the death of him.*
4. A manner of dying: *a heroine's death.*
5. Often **Death** A personification of the destroyer of life, usually represented as a skeleton holding a scythe.
6.
   a. Bloodshed; murder.
   b. Execution.
7. *Law-* Civil death.
8. The termination or extinction of something: *the death of imperialism.*

Main Entry: **do**
Function: *verb*
Inflected Forms: **did; done; doing; does**
transitive verb **1** : PERFORM, EXECUTE
2 : COMMIT <*did* this act of cruelty> verbal auxiliary —used
with the infinitive without *to* go form present and past tenses in legal
and parliamentary language <*do* hereby bequeath>—**do business** :
to be engaged in business activities (as soliciting sales); *specifically*
: to engage in activities sufficient to subject a foreign company to
the personal jurisdiction of a state <was sufficient to constitute *doing
business* in the state —*International Shoe Company v. Washington,*
326 U.S. 310 (1945)> —see also DOING BUSINESS STATUTE

us   (ŭs)
pron. The objective form of we.

1. Used as the direct object of a verb: *She saw us on the subway.*
2. Used as the indirect object of a verb: *They offered us free tickets to the show.*
3. Used as the object of a preposition: *This letter is ad- is addressed to us.*
4. *Informal.* Used as a predicate nominative: *It's us.* See Usage Note at we.
5. *Nonstandard.* Used reflexively as the indirect object of a verb: *We decided to get us another car.* See note at me.

part (pärt)
n.

1. A portion, division, piece, or segment of a whole.
2. Any of several equal portions or fractions that can con- constitute a whole or into which a whole can be divided: *a mixture of two parts flour to one part sugar.*
3. A division of a literary work: *a novel in three parts.*
4. A division of a literary work: *a novel in three parts.*
    a. An organ, member, or other division of an organism: *A tail is not a part of a guinea pig.*

b. **Parts** The external genitals.

5. A component that can be separated from or attached to a system; a detachable piece: *spare parts for cars.*
6. A role: *He has the main part in the play.*
7. One's responsibility, duty, or obligation; share: *We each do our part to keep the house clean.*
8. Individual endowment or ability; talent. Often used in the plural.
9. A region, area, land, or territory. Often use in the plural: "Minding your own business is second nature in these parts" (Boston).
10. The line where the hair on the head is parted.
11. Music.
    a. The music or score for a particular instrument, as in an orchestra.
    b. One of the melodic divisions or voices of a contrapuntal composition.

v. **parted, parting, parts**
v. tr.

1. To divide or break into separate parts.
2. To break up (a relationship) by separating the elements involved: *parted company.*
3. To put or keep apart: *No one could part the two friends.*
4. To comb (hair, for example) away from a dividing line, as on the scalp.
5. <u>Archaic.</u> To divide into shares or portions.

v. intr.

1. To become divided or separated: *The curtain parted in the middle.*
2. To go apart from one another; separate: *They parted as friends. They were forced to part from one another.*
See Synonyms at separate.

3. To separate or divide into ways going in different directions: *The road parts about halfway into the for the forest.*
4. To go away; depart.
5. To disagree by factions: *The committee parted over the issue of pay raises for employees.*
6. <u>Archaic.</u> To die.

or¹ (ôr; ər *when unstressed*)
conj.

1.
   a. Used to indicate an alternative, usually only before the last term of a series: *hot or cold; this, this, that, or the other.*
   b. Used to indicate the second of two alternatives, the first being preceded by *either* or *whether: Your answer is either ingenious or wrong. I I didn't know whether to laugh or cry.*
   c. <u>Archaic.</u> Used to indicate the first of two alternatives, with the force of *either* or *whether.*
2. Used to indicate a synonymous or equivalent expression: *acrophobia, or fear of great heights.*
3. Used to indicate uncertainty or indefiniteness: *two or three.*

as¹ (ăz; əz *when unstressed*)
adv.

1. To the same extent or degree; equally: *The child sang as sweetly as a nightingale.*
2. For instance: *large carnivores, as the bear or lion.*
3. When taken into consideration in a specified relation or form: *this definition as distinguished from the second one.*

conj.

1. To the same degree or quantity that. Often used as a correlative after *so* or *as: You are as sweet as sugar. The situation is not so bad as you suggest.*
2. In the same manner or way that: *Think as I think.*

3. At the same time that; while: *slipped on the ice as I ran home.*
4. For the reason that; because: *went to bed early, as I was exhausted.*
5. With the result that: *He was so foolish as to lie.*
6. Though: *Great as the author was, he proved a bad model. Ridiculous as it seems, the tale is true.*
7. In accordance with which or with the way in which: *The hotel is quite comfortable as such establishments go. The sun is hot, as everyone knows.*
8. *Informal.* That: *I don't know as I can answer your question.*

long¹ (lông, lŏng)
adj. **longer, longest**

1.
    a. Extending or traveling a relatively great distance.
    b. Having relatively great height; tall.
    c. Having the greater length of two or the greatest length of several: *the long edge of the door.*
2. Of relatively great duration: *a long time.*
3. Of a specified linear extent or duration: *a mile long; an hour long.*
4. Made up of many members or items: *a long shopping list.*
5.
    a. Extending beyond an average or standard: *a long game.*
    b. Extending or landing beyond a given boundary, limit, or goal: *Her first serve was long.*
6. Tediously protracted; lengthy: *a long speech.*
7. Concerned with distant issues; far-reaching: *took a long view of the geopolitical issues.*
8. Involving substantial chance; risky: *long odds.*
9. Having an abundance or excess of: "politicians whose résumés are long on competence" (Margaret Garrard Warner).
10. Having a holding of a commodity or security in expectation of a rise in price: *long on soybeans.*

11.
  a. *Linguistics.* Having a comparatively great duration. Used of a vowel or consonant.
  b. *Grammar.* Of, relating to, or being a vowel sound in English, such as the vowel sound (ā) in *mate* or (ē) *feet,* that is descended from a vowel of long duration.
12.
  a. Stressed or accented. Used of a syllable in accentual prosody.
  b. Being of relatively great duration. Used of a syllable in quantitative prosody.

we (wē)
pron.

1. Used by the speaker or writer to indicate the speaker or writer along with another or others as the subject: *We made it to the lecture hall on time. We are planning a trip to Arizona this winter.*
2. Used to refer to people in general, including the speaker or writer: "How can we enter the professions and yet remain civilized human beings?" (Virginia Woolf).
3. Used instead of *I,* especially by a writer wishing to reduce or avoid a subjective tone.
4. Used instead of *I,* especially by an editorialist, in expressing the opinion or point of view of a publication's management.
5. Used instead of *I* by a sovereign in formal address to refer to himself or herself.
6. Used instead of *you* in direct address, especially to imply a patronizing camaraderie with the addressee: *How are we feeling today?*

both (bōth)
adj.

One and the other; relating to or being two in conjunction: *Both guests have arrived. Both the books are torn. Both her fingers are broken.*

pron.

The one and the other: *Both were candidates. We are both candidates. Both of us are candidates.*

conj.

Used with *and* to indicate that each of two things in a coordinated phrase or clause is included: *both men and women; an attorney well regarded for both intelligence and honesty.*

shall (shăl)
aux.v. past tense **should** (sho͝od)

1. Used before a verb in the infinitive to show:
    a. Something that will take place or exist in the future: *We shall arrive tomorrow.*
    b. Something, such as an order, promise, requirement, or obligation: *You shall leave now. He shall answer for his misdeeds. The penalty shall not exceed two years in prison.*
    c. They will to do something or have something take place: *I shall go out if I feel like it.*
    d. Something that is inevitable: *That day shall come.*
2. <u>Archaic.</u>
    a. To be able to.
    b. To have to; must.

live[1] (lĭv)

v. **lived, living, lives**
v. intr.

1. To be alive; exist.
2. To continue to be alive: *lived through a bad accident.*
3. To support oneself; subsist: *living on rice and fish; lives on a small inheritance.*
4. To reside; dwell: *lives on a farm.*

5. To conduct one's life in a particular manner: *lived frugally.*
6. To pursue a positive, satisfying existence; enjoy life:
life: *those who truly live.*
7. To remain in human memory: *an event that lives on in our minds.*

v. tr.
1. To spend or pass (one's life).
2. To go through; experience: *lived a nightmare.*
3. To practice in one's life: *live one's beliefs.*

Now after a couple reexamines the value of one's vows, they should have a clearer cognizance of nearly every word or event that took place on their wedding day? Remembering one's vows after years of marriage, should allow a person to question their own loyalty; whether their vows were from their lips or their heart!

As a person reevaluates their vows, it has caused many to realize the actual impact of God's presence.

The Bible mentions some obligations that man find hard to honor. That's why pastors should introduce marriage vows prior to Couples, weeks before preceding the marriage. Such practice will certainly give a couple plenty of time to understand the degree of their commitments. They should carefully scrutinize the depth of matrimony prior to an appointed marriage day. The couple should approach a marriage with the greatest of caution as they would heedfully select a family insurance plan!

In this new age we need to take marriage more seriously, and get away from the Hollywood style, which have left many traumatized.

For a reminder most people do not realize the power of words pronounced at weddings. Probably because of the lack of understanding the significance of God's role within a marriage, that our vows are actually centered on His will. A person's vow is a commitment to God concerning their spouse.

Vows are very precious in God's sight, so if a person make a vow, they should do their very best to complete it.

What does a vow mean to you?

Deuteronomy 23:21
"When thou shalt vow a vow unto the LORD thy God, thou shalt not slack to pay it: for the LORD thy God will surely require it of thee; and it would be sin in thee".

Thou shalt not be slack to pay it, lest if it be delayed beyond the first opportunity the zeal abates, the vow be forgotten, or something happen to disable thee for the performance of it. *That which has gone out of thy lips* as a solemn and deliberate vow must not be recalled, but *thou shalt keep and perform it,* punctually and fully". The rule of the gospel goes somewhat further than this. *Every one, according as he purposeth in his heart,* though it have not gone out of his lips, *so let him give.* Here is a good reason why we should pay our vows, that if we do not *God will require it of us,* will surely and severely reckon with us, not only for lying, but to vainly for attempting to mock him, who cannot be mocked.

Ecclesiastes 5:4-5
"When thou vowest a vow unto God, defer not to pay it; for *he hath* no pleasure in fools: pay that which thou hast vowed". "Better *is it* that thou shouldest not vow, than that thou shouldest vow and not pay".

A vow is a bond upon the soul by which we solemnly oblige ourselves, not only, in common, to do that which we are already bound to do, but, in some meticulous instances, to do that which we were not under any antecedent obligation, whether it respects honoring God or serving the interests of his kingdom among men. When under the sense of some affliction, or in the pursuit of some mercy, thou hast vowed such a vow as this *unto God,* know that *thou hast opened thy mouth unto the Lord and thou canst not go back;* therefore, pay it; perform what thou hast promised; bring to God what thou hast dedicated and devoted to him: *Pay that which thou hast vowed;* pay it in full and *keep not back any part of the price;* pay it in kind, do not *alter it or change it,* so the law was. Have we vowed to *give our own selves unto the Lord?* Let us then be as good as our word, act in his service, to his glory, and not sacrilegiously alienate ourselves. *Defer not to pay it.* If it be in the power of thy hands to pay it today, leave it not till tomorrow; do not *beg a day,* nor put it off to a more convenient season. By delay the sense of the obligation slackens and cools, and is in danger of wearing off; we thereby discover a loathness and backwardness to perform our vow; and *qui non est hodie cras minus aptus erit–he who is not inclined today will be averse tomorrow.* The longer it is put off the more difficult it will be to bring ourselves to it; death may not only prevent the payment, but fetch thee to judgment, under the guilt of a broken vow.

Two reasons are given here why we should speedily and cheerfully pay our vows: Because otherwise we affront God; we play the fool with him, as if we designed to put a trick upon him; and *God has no pleasure in fools.* More is implied than is expressed; the meaning is, He greatly abhors such fools and such unwise dealings. *Has he need of fools?* No; *be not deceived, God is not mocked,* but will surely and severely reckon with those that thus play fast and loose with him. Because otherwise we wrong ourselves, we lose the benefit of the making of the *vow,* nay, we incur the penalty for the breach of it; so that it would have been better a great deal *not to have vowed,* more safe and more to our advantage, than to *vow and not to pay.* Not to have *vowed* would have been but an omission, but to *vow and not pay* incurs the guilt of treachery and perjury; it is *lying to God,*

The first marriage vows: Eve was made especially for Adam. This was the first marriage. That is why Jesus reminded the people that the meaning of marriage dependent on the origin of marriage and the first marriage is in Genesis (Adam and Eve)

"And he answered and said unto them, have ye not read that he which made them at the beginning made them male and female, and said, for this cause shall a man leave father and mother, and shall cleave to his wife: and they two shall be one flesh? Wherefore they are no more two, but one flesh. What therefore God hath united together, let no man put asunder".

Chapter 3

==========

FAIRYTALE WEDDING

A fairytale wedding is basely a false conception of a matrimonial-union made in heaven, without having the full understanding of all the responsibilities by which a marriage requires. A fairytale wedding can be perceived by individuals who confuses reality with fiction, or fantasy with dreams; an imaginary fabrication which dwells within the subconscious of the misinformed.

It is easy to picture a perfect marriage, whereas the big question should be asked is how can a person have a perfect union between two dysfunctional people? It is true that we're all subject to error in one area or another, frequently believing everything is all-right when it's not.

For a reminder, any person can look good at the alter, or coming down the isle throwing the garter belt, or riding in a limousine. Yes, this looks and sounds great, but in reality it bears a much greater responsibility.

The fairytale wedding is when individuals go into a marriage thinking that it's heaven-bound, and that all of their problems are immediately solved!

Note: Never would have imagined going thru:

      a. Married and Lonely days
      b. Confused days

c. Tears shed
d. Heart ache and pained
e. Misunderstanding
f. Silent days
g. Days you just feel abandon
h. No good night kiss
i. No encouragements
j. No sex
k. No trust
l. No meals
m. No bath water
n. Days you just do not want to be bothered
o. No greeting
p. No hugs
q. No phone calls
r. Hard times
s. Struggles
t. Disagreement
u. Argument
v. No love
w. No peace
x. Feel like given up
y. Feel like divorcing
z. No nagging
aa. No help
bb. Ups and downs
cc. sprit of controlling

When most people imagine a fairytale wedding, they mostly dwell on the glamour instead of the obligation it carries. A fairytale wedding is a wedding which individuals feel they can predict its outcome; along with failing to acknowledge that only God is the nucleus of one's destiny.

In a fairytale wedding our faith level is at an all time high. We often sit and picture how good life will be, instead of dealing with some of the struggles life carries. I'm sure that many of us as children have imagined a marriage without its share of struggles: no lonely days or ups and down, no tears, heart aches or pain.

Here is an example: many of us often focus on, fancy passing cars, quoting: "That's going to be my car." Yet again as a child I personally imagined those same cars to be mine when became an adult, not considering that the model of those cars would have changed!

For another example, as a youth, I had pictured my wife in my mind before meeting her. I pictured her shape, her skin complexion, the way she would smile, the tone of her voice, height and so on. Well, after twenty-years of marriage, I discovered that a lot of my childhood expectations became reality, but required some extra efforts to become a dream. A childhood dream without a commitment to build those dreams will set an adult up for utter failure!

Many of our parents have laid the foundation of how we should live in a marriage. They have taught us what to do, but can never teach us what they themselves haven't experienced. Let's face it; the final journey of a marriage rests solely upon a couple's personal divine commitment, which at often times means going beyond the call of duty.

Much of our mythical beliefs have also evolved from our parents, who have failed to inform us about the other side of marriage. They have covered-up a lot of their own missed steps, which have misled many to follow a troubled path, which could have been avoided.

Conclusively the fairytale wedding is exactly what it says, a fabled belief! It starts with the bride's gown having the long train, the groom with the latest tux, and the fancy cars or the big limousines, the gigantic wedding party, the admirable cake, gifts, card, a couple's portrait in the news journal, etc., etc. Naturally, with people from all walks of life ever cheering you on.

What about the planned honeymoon trip to the islands of your choice, along with your endless prayers to never-never let such romance end. Living in a true fantasy world to evade the real you and reality.

Fairytale means: **fairy-tale** (fâr'ē-tāl)
adj.

1. Of or relating to a fairy tale. **Fairytale**
n1: a story about fairies; told to amuse children [syn: fairy tale, fairy story] 2: an interesting but highly implausible story; often told as an excuse [syn: fairy tale, fairy story, cock-and-bull story, song and dance]

fairytale

Main Entry: **Fairy tale**
Function: noun

1. a story (as for children) involving fantastic forces and beings (as fairies, wizards, and goblins)–called also fairy story.
2. a made-up story usually designed to mislead married people who never believed in a fairytale wedding. It's a made up story designed to mislead you and set you and your spouse up for failure.

Every thing in life comes with a price tag and that's reality. Our marriages are tested at work, with family, at home and so on.
Our marriage is tested because of the power that comes with a marriage.
The devil has been fighting against marriages since the days of Adams and Eve. The Tempter caught Eve when she was alone, making it difficult for her to run back to her husband to get a more accurate plan.
Adams and his wife Eve should have been on one accord, in mind body and soul. But when a person is married and lonely the devil's objective is to keep on kicking until he destroys that matrimony. Lucifer manipulates the human spirit, if a marriage is not based around a fairytale. The marriage will continue to disintegrate as long as the devil dictates its course. The Deceiver will destroy a marriage by coaching the conscious to find a better or perfect mate. How deceptive, because there exist no perfect person or wedding,

since a matrimony is centered on a personal commitment, based upon God's guidance.

So if a person goes into a relationship having the mind set of a perfect wedding, then it becomes a situation of setting him or her up for failure. This naturally happens, if the person leaves no room for God to operate.

Chapter 4

NEED CHANGE BACK

Have you gone to the store and bought something, and after purchasing, asked yourself have I paid too much for this and should demand some change back? Needing your change back is when a person is trapped in a relationship that doesn't measure up to his or her expectation. Now, some people are experiencing loneliness and unhappiness in their marriage, where in retrospect, is patiently waiting to be salaried for their distresses, another way of saying: "Return my change!" I'm sure that we have heard of couples, who have gone to great extent for the care of others. But when it comes to their own mates, bizarrely to say, one of the spouses may strangely station themselves at the register with their hands stretched out for services they may feel they have earned.

Many couples believe they deserve more out of their marriage than what life has offered, and that they will never feel justified until their needs have been honored. This desire to be compensated for services linked to a relationship can be arbitrarily resolved by consulting a counselor, not necessarily one's best friend, mom or dad, but having a direct spiritual connection with the "Redeemer". A person must be wise as well as smart by carefully making the right decisions toward solving their differences. One of the worse moves any couple can make is to publicly broadcast their problems before privately resolving them. It is wise to say, that it takes time to solve or ease any form of discomfort within a person's private life.

Lots of sicknesses evolving within a person's physical and mental world often occurs from relationships having stress, depression, oppression and every other discomforted condition, along with our own false imaginary delusion about life. We must stop feeling that our marriages are exempted from any form of failure, disappointments, embarrassments or negatives. We must accept that what a person puts into a marriage is what he shall harvest!

To have a good harvest we must certainly exercise prayer to acquire God's total guidance. Marriage has always had its ups and downs throughout the history of man. But regardless of such, it has always had its benefit of life's fulfillment.

For a couple to get their moneys worth from a troubled marriage, they should strive to understanding the principal of teamwork, and stop taking each other for granted. The day a person says "I do," is the day their investment begins, which is like a 401K plan where everyday one's investments bring about one's prosperity, which greatly rely upon teamwork. There exists an order of uniqueness in every marriage if approached mannerly. Couples should never directly base their marriages upon the experience of others. They should face reality and quickly break away from a lot of fixed social customs, and approach life with a long range goal. They must eliminate their hopes for a quick-fix that rests upon a short lived dream, realizing that a marriage is an everyday learning experience! New acquaintance should be briefed a thousand times over that compatibility is a key essential in preserving a companion-ship. Realizing that if there are great differences in their courtship, then there will exist an even greater difference in their marriage. They should be briefed that if a couple can't work as a team before a wedding, then it is nine times out of ten that they will not accomplish such a goal after the wedding. Couples should be made alerted not to wait until after their wedding to seek compatibility, but strongly investigate such harmonious attractions prior to walking down the isles. They should never forget the old saying, that what you see is what you get!

It doesn't matter what clothes a person wears, the way they fix their hair, or how they dress, because no matter how he or she style themselves, they will still remain the same.

A person should know the difference between lusts and love, before asking for compensation in reference to a bad marriage. A person's lust is like the four seasons of a year, it comes and goes. A person's itch never remain the same; it's an unstable experience and difficult to keep track of. However, it is the power of love that has the potency to weather any storm. The truest form of love demonstrates respect. It doesn't matter how a person look, the length of their hair or how well their bodies are shaped. Love evaluates those aspects as non-sensible! Now the major question should be asked, where are some individuals in their relationship? Is it love or lust?

Some people are so lonely in their marriage, that they have lost track of who they really are. Many have taken on fictitious characters to satisfy their mates; a portrayal so well acted out that it should have won them an Academy, Oscar or a Grammy award! What an experience of matrimony; married but still feel empty, neglected and despaired! Not knowing which way to turn, since all they can recall in their conscious, is a committed vow "I do;" an oath which has for many years lost its appeal. How sad to acknowledge that in reality their marriage is just an act of going through the motions.

There is a solution for every marital crisis if couples knew what buttons to push or not push. It truly involves numerous factors, from praying, planning, meditating, compromising, etc. But in many cases such efforts can be too late, since many couples have suffered alienation for so long. They just want to say goodbye, cash in, and divide the profits.

A person's main objective is to please their spouse; realizing that their bodies are no longer their sole possession. Every couple should ask themselves if they understand the most vital methods to uplift their spouse. Because when a spouse fails to meet his or her personal obligation, then it is possible that someone else can replace his position. But in all good common sense, God can prevail against any odds in our spiritual battles if we offer an unconditional surrender to Jesus Christ!

It is not surprising that the divorce rates are so modernly high. Remember, God is scarce in our lives; we lack spiritual guidance, hope and faith, which are the very fabrics to sustain a family structure; the back bone of a nation. We have definitely failed to understand that we are fighting wickedness and principalities instead of flesh and blood (Eph. 6:12). Our true enemies are not ourselves.

It appears that a spiritual battle in a marriage is one of the worst battles a person can experience, because someone is sure to come out wounded, hurt, or even dead.

A marriage can be a traumatic spiritual battle, because it attacks the very heart of one's faith or belief system; devastating the most sensitive areas by which the natural eye could never have foretold. In a regular battle, a person may have an idea of who their enemy is his or her location, nationality and type of weaponry they bear. But in a spiritual warfare, which chiefly involves a chaotic conflict within the inner soul of an individual, is certainly devastating to the human psyche! A raging fight that never ceases; a battle that is strong enough to kill, or maim children, animals, wife and husband. This is a vicious struggle that will leave homes in an utter ruin.

The mass destruction in a spiritual marital battle is when a person begins to lose their mind, hope, faith in God, and even the will to live by violently removing one's self from life's existence.

Imagine a person buying something and got the wrong change back. That's how some marriages are; they love their spouse, but also have a love someone else. Sometime relationships never officially end, but separate with unfinished business, having their hearts knitted more to their ex-lover than to their own spouse. Such experiences have continued throughout an individual's life.

Chapter 5

========

TIME TO SCREAM

How do you know when its time to scream? Well, it's time to scream when you find yourself going through the same old day by day involvements, when nothing new comes out of it; an experience that only perpetrates frustration and confusion. A situation which leaves a person in a state of melancholy! A state where a person doesn't know if they are going and coming or laughing or crying.

Sometimes the only person who realizes what is actually going on in a marriage is the participant and God. When a person seeks to do all what they know to preserve their wedding, as they pray, fast, and read all types of biblical Scriptures, just to realize that nothing is seemingly to change their lives, will naturally upset anyone. Imagine a person wanting more attention, affection and friends, and not able to acquire these magnificent emergencies. This could generate an unresisting desire to loudly scream.

Let's face it; it's alright to scream to find that ultimate relief! Another form of relief is when a person talk to someone they are comfortable with, who is not necessarily a family member. Sometimes it is best to confide in a stranger, such as counselor, who won't become bias if a person is married or single.

During a marriage some people are more in love with the ceremony than the wedding itself, which is dangerous because the ceremony ends after the comment: "I do." After the remark "I do," everyone goes home, the tux has been returned, the dress has been hung up, and the garter belt has been thrown, as reality slowly sits in.

Couples should stop playing games with each other. It is often within a marriage where couples are unhappy. Their ill-behaviors are often demonstrated in their character of loneliness, sleeping in separate beds rooms, because of their disagreements in the relationship.

Scream until you let it all out! Scream until the walls of Jericho comes falling down. Release your frustration. Scream-scream!

> Walls of pain
> Walls of doubt
> Walls of pressure
> Walls of confusion
> Walls of mental break down
> Walls of suicide
> Walls of hurt
> Walls of resentment
> Walls of fear
> Walls of struggles
> Walls of forgiveness
> Walls of trust
> Walls of anger
> Walls of honesty
> Walls of jealousy
> Walls of envy
> Walls of withdrawal
> Wall of stress
> Wall of guilt
> Walls of loneliness
> Walls of anxiety
> Walls of oppression
> Walls of suppression
> Walls of bitterness

Chapter 6

========

MALE CHAUVINIST

A person may ask what a male chauvinism has to do with marriage and loneliness. Well, a male chauvinist is a jealous and controlling person, who often suspects his wife of cheating or having an extra marital affair. Male chauvinist insecurity is his worst enemy. He has many hang-ups, by which one does not believe that a woman should be a pastor, or show any leadership. This character of a chauvinist is thoroughly exhibited in the earlier section of this book.

A female during a courtship can see much of a man's controlling attitude, but mystically chose to condone his character, until the final boiling point. Some of the signs of male chauvinist are located in the below column.

    A. The husband begins to verbally abuse his spouse.
    B. Attack her verbally.
    C. Attack her mentally.
    D. Screen her cell phone calls.
    E. He will time your work schedule.
    F. Call you all day to keep track of you.
    G. He will follow you around the city.
    H. Check her cell phone bill.
    I. Try hard to smell a man's cologne on your clothes and body.

J. He Look for marks on her neck and back.
K. He will check her underwear for sperm.
L. Never trust you as a woman.
M. Will not respect you as a woman.

Oh yes, women today often look over the fault of their men's chauvinist, because of love, which makes a lot of people do some crazy things. Women see the signs, but hesitate to take action to avoid the chance of losing that special someone in their lives. Lovers often see their differences following the wedding date. But as mentioned, their abnormal behavior was there all the time, but was over looked by both parties, because of their attraction for one another; as often stated, "Love is blind."

Male chauvinist

A male chauvinist is a man who demand and command authority over women. Woman must look for the signs of a male chauvinist in the early stages of their courtship. Their disadvantage is when they label all guys as dogs-chauvinist, failing to accept that there are some good guys out there.

Through research it has been proven that a male chauvinist will not admit his brutal acts, such denial has made a lot of women feel worthless, having no real meaning in their lives.

A lot of males chauvinist comes from a person's up bringing, learned from another male. They love the control, the bragging rights, and the power to make all decisions in the home. They love the authority of being the big man, the king, priest and prophet of their homes. Remember these comments? "I do what I want, when I want and how I want". "I come and go when I please". Many demand their spouses to remain home and pregnant, and always ready to serve them. A male chauvinist is taught not to compromise with their wives or any other woman, but to dominate them! A lot of their behavior comes from the injuries or hurt they themselves have acquired during childhood, probably from their own mothers. The truth about it is that a male chauvinist really doesn't respect women, and will likely treat his pets better than his wife. His main objective is to tear his wife and every other female around him down to nothing. His ultimate goal is to destroy a woman's will, not physically but mentally and emotionally, where the victim's own family will not recognize her. His aim is to destroy her self esteem to the point of lacking the capacity to care for her own children; a condition that usually sends a sane person insane!

A male chauvinist usually enters into a relationship with a preconceived expectation about what he wants, and not what his female companion wants. Once again, he comments: I'm the man of this house and you will do what I say, "I have the first and last word and make all the decisions".

The male chauvinist feeds off of the beliefs of other male chauvinists. They've been taught not to relent in their ways; either it's their way or the highway!

A real man loves his wife and often shares her ideas. He understands that he is the head, but that the head is limited without the neck. That is to say that a wife's opinion can represent a vital view, which can turn an unfavorable situation favorable. It takes wisdom to see a close hidden view, and when a couple marries, and then every view, including the woman's is essential in keeping the marriage healthy.

One of the worst things about a marriage is when only one party is authorized to makes the major decisions for the entire family.

In the bible Abraham listens to his wife Sarah when asked to remove a son he loved from the household. Abraham under-stood that God speaks to the woman as well as to the man during family crisis, especially when one party is heading in the wrong direction. That is why men must have a spiritual wife, who can hear the voice of God when the husband is out of touch. For example, Adam's frequency was so out of touch with God that his actions remain to have a profound affect on today's marriages. It may have reversed had Eve chose an alternative approach, by listening to God rather than the serpent. What a disaster when both parties are out of touch with the spiritual realm.

In the eyes of a male chauvinist, any man who seek advice from his wife is not considered a real man, but a hen pecked-wimp and soft.

A spiritual man loves Jesus, not just by lip service but through his divine performance. A Holy man will seek the Lord for advice on how to love his wife through thick and thin. He does not view his wife's advice as flexing his muscles, or ruling the home! A sound minded man will understand that a good wife knows who the head of the house is without being scoffed and scorned! He cherishes the thought that his children and wife respects him as a wonderful leader by listening to the whole family.

Now many women are lonely in their marriages because they live in fear from abusive relationships. But what they must understand is that there are plenty of help in our society for victims of abuse.

Some chauvinists are so dominant that a person who visits their residents wouldn't believe that a woman ever lived in the premises, because all the furniture appears to have a masculine style. The male chauvinist doesn't recognize his woman as a queen, but only a piece of meat, and believes he knows the best way to cook it. How sad that he gets away with it only because he can!

Some women ought to get themselves together and lift their heads high. They should go shopping and change their whole out look about life, realizing that they are beautiful, even when they're not told by their own spouses. The woman ought to develop a new outlook by changing her dress code. She should alter her hair style and cloth design, which will send a strong message that she has found a new identity. It is necessary that she assure her husband that life is not all about him, that there is more to her than what he observes. She must convince him that there must be an immediate change if they're going to maintain cohesiveness. Yes, it's time for a change if the marriage is to survive! Either they work together or separate, realizing that they can avoid going in separate ways if they work as a team.

It is not prudent for women to believe that all men are dogs. The majority of men desire a peaceful strong wife. Not a nagging woman, but a wife who will cover his back. It is the male chauvinist who desires the good old house slave, and if any female fits this description, and then they should seek professional help.

Chapter 7

WOMAN CHAUVINIST

The majority of men would love to have a strong woman in their corner at all times, a woman who will support their interest. Some men measure their wives according to the character of their moms. They enjoy matching their wife's cooking, sewing and other behavior with their moms. They realize that Jezebel was an unusual character, which their sisters and moms wouldn't prefer for them to bring home. The story of Jezebel is branded in the turbulent period of the divided kingdom of Israel. She was a Negress Queen of Israel and wife of King Ahab. Jezebel's ambition was to oppose God with a new worshiping system called Baalism. She ruled Israel for over forty-years, before being overthrown by Jehu, who demanded her eunuchs to cast her from a chamber. The saga of Jezebel is related to several major issues:

- A conflict between the worshipers of the emerging God Yahweh, and of the traditional gods Baal and Asherah.
- The nature of kingship, and limits on the power of the monarch.

Jezebel was the daughter of Ethbaal, king of the Zidonians or Tyrians. King Ahab of Israel, the son of Omri, who did evil in the sight of God, took Jezebel in marriage, and accepted the worshiping of Baal. Ahab coveted the vineyard of Naboth, but when he failed to seize it, Jezebel had Naboth stoned, which enabled Ahab to possess the vineyard. It was following this incident that Jezebel introduced the worshiping of Astarte and Baalism to Israel. She then slewed the prophets of the Lord, and hides many in a cave with only water and bread. Jezebel is modernly referred as a woman chauvinist, the mother of harlots and abominations of the earth. She led her husband into the same idolatry, and fed the prophets of Baal at her table.

The name Jezebel means "Where is the prince?" The Jezebel spirit has manifested itself in the world to the highest pinnacles of government. The prophecy of tribulation is in these last days, and has already engulfed the greater part of Christendom. Today's Christian churches has allowed Jezebel's idolatry to pollute many hearts and minds, and subsequently all other facet of society.

Jezebel was a whore and a witch whose spirit endures throughout the world. She covered her face with make-up to appear more attractive to lure God's favorites. Jezebel was a woman who was destroyed by the very government she corrupted. The word of God came to Elijah to address Ahab concerning the state of his affairs throughout Israel. The prophet Elijah appeared out of nowhere stirring the hearts of the righteous, and afterward witnessing the priests of Baal killed by the people. It was not Elijah alone but Jehu the King of Israel, who sought to demolish the prophets of Baal; seriously avenging the blood of God's sends prophets. It was Jehu who demanded the death of Jezebel to be hurled from a chamber. In the end, Jehu like Jezebel didn't follow the laws of God; a continuous practice by today's Christians. It is up to the church to become the spotless bride and cast out today's false doctrine. The churches have the right and power to take on such responsibility.

Different demons have different names. The Jezebel demonic spirits entices God's servants to fornication, and to commit adultery. Attitudes are contrived to try to cover-up the sins of the world, and the true prophetic spirit of God. The sins of fornication include any sexual act outside of marriage. The New Testament identifies fornication as a punishable act. Fornication is not limited to an act of sex, but is also described as any action that disconnects itself from the principals of God, since Jesus is wedded to the church! When Jesus condemns those who have committed adultery with the Satanism of Jezebel, He is referring to the church and its worldliness, not necessarily the act of physical sex! Jezebel remains to be a world political figure, who continues to control and manipulation the good will of man. Once under this delusion, the spirit of Jezebel entices the mind of the innocent into captivity. Her deceptive disguises perpetuate the worse form of demoralization.

The spirit of Jezebel's influence has misled God's people to serve a corrupted church system in opposition to God. Instead of being the bride of Christ, the church has transformed itself into a harlot to chase the pollution of the world. It has been modernly difficult for the so called Christians to resist Jezebel's demonic spell. Let's face it, those who have been captured by her lure continues to live in a false state of delusion. Jezebel is the spirit of a modern day Babylon. The bible has warned man to have no ties with her diabolic rituals, a warning that many pastors faithfully observe.

The spirit of Elijah that opposes the spirit of Jezebel is prophetic. However, those pastors who will not submit to the will of God have found themselves between a rock and a hard place. Their decision to corroborate with the evilness of this world, will surely earn them a place far outside the Kingdom of God. These so called pastors have for so long manipulated the public to serve their own greedy habits. They have time after time tried to convince the church to convert the ill-virtue to righteousness. Ever persuading their congregation that what is considered to be evil is actually right. How sad!

Once again it is the Jezebel spirit that has seduced our present generation to commit fornication, whether sexually or politically to defy God. Those who are under Jezebel's hypnotic-spell have convinced themselves that their choice to honor her influence will be pardoned by God. They have lost their zeal of faith, and are certainly bounded for the lake of hell. Those helpless followers of Jezebel definitely need all the prayers one could give.

Woman Chauvinist
A woman chauvinist is a female who believes men are innately inferior to woman.

n : a woman with a chauvinistic belief of the inferiority of men [syn: sexist]

Men beware.

Once again what is a woman chauvinist? A woman chauvinist is a female who feels she has to be in complete control over a man's world. She loves her man, but dishonors the position he holds, even though his position was authorized by God! A female chauvinist is usually a woman who was raised by another female.

A female chauvinist's mother sets the agenda of how young girls should act. The female chauvinist's mother regularly develops her own house rules, and not the husband's. She conducts the same behavior in her marriage as witnessing her mother's behavior. The husband of a female chauvinist goes along with his wife's decisions in order to keep peace in the home. He feels that if he doesn't consent to her wishes, then he may be deprived of sexual rights.

The woman chauvinist will insist to make all the arrangements in the home. She selects all the furniture, what car the family should have, even to the point of telling her man how to style his hair, and what type of cloths to wear.

The female chauvinist pay all of the bills and instructs the household what to do, believing that a man's chore is to work a job, cut the grass, paint the house and baby sit! In ancient biblical times the man was normally out in the field, or fighting wars, while the woman raised the children, and took on other domestic responsibilities. Nevertheless, in today's society such chores have been reversed, leaving the woman as the head of the house! In the spiritual realm, this type of marriage has its flaws, but all things are possible with God, therefore, such conditions through prayer can be properly resolved.

It is not a mistake to declare the woman as a queen of her mansion. But she should question her own motives to hold both positions as Queen and King! This reverse in authority ship is in defiance to God's design of the family structure. It is critical that the man acts swiftly to restore the roll of a leadership, realizing that the buck stops with him.

Some women chauvinists have so much family power that when the couple goes shopping, the woman will purposely ignore the husband's choice and opinion on certain home necessities. Her husband's thoughts are routinely shot down! The woman chauvinist is so dominant that she often looks for a weak man that she can control.

She looks for a man that she can intimidate, and if he doesn't like it than he's told to "Hit the road Jack and don't you come back no more," especially if he makes less money than she does.

A reminder of what brings about a woman chauvinist is rather fascinating. Most female chauvinists are orientated at an early age by their mother's atrocious behavior to wrestle the power from the hands of their husbands.

One technique applied to control a home is orchestrated through sex. The woman can become pretty repugnant when a man desires to have sex. Think on these remarks: "My head hurts," "I'm too tired," "I'm not in the mood". "You just had some last week." So like Esau, some men are willing to give up their birth rights for certain emergencies. However, when a woman wants to make love to a man, he usually consents, knowing that if he doesn't, it's quite possible that another party will replace him. Men are better at waiting than women, because they're so use to hearing the phrase "No, not tonight!"

In many instances a spouse can force another into infidelity. Remember this saying, "No it's not right in the site of God to have sex that way". How many times have we heard that comment? It is dangerous to believe that a spouse should have full possession of his or her own body. It is not wise to believe that a party is doing the other a favor by making love, because when one fails to satisfy the other, then someone outside the marriage can make up the difference.

A lack of communication within a marriage can definitely be a fiasco. A couple should never believe that a spouse is so much in love with Jesus that they won't cheat. Let's be serious, cheating happens everyday!

Many women acknowledge that their husbands are Pastors, working for God. They understand his chores and other ministries that he is responsible for. Nevertheless, the wives also realize that their husband's first duty is to manage their homes. This has not always been easy, due to their over-worked schedule. Many Pastors are so caught-up in their churches, until they have slacked on giving their own homes the care it requires. Strangely enough to say, but if some Pastors would run their homes as well as their churches, then many of their marriages would survive. The Pastors invest so much time into other people's business, until they find little time for their own families. After going home from church, some Pastors are so fatigued until it's difficult to give their own families quality time; in all likelihood based on a critical imbalance of judgment. In a marriage a person must understand how to honor God, without smothering their own families.

The order of God's business is to first recognize Him, then the family, followed by the church.

Not the church first, but God and family which makes a church. Our God is a God of complete order, meaning that there can be no church without a family structure.

Man has carelessly put more time into his secular jobs than into his marriage. He has a habit of working over time, going to college, trade school and buying dozens of books concerning job opportunities. When was the last time, any of us can remember buying a book on How to love, or take a college course on How to please our Mates?

The female Jezebel chauvinist is ever alive, desiring full control within a domicile. The wicked Jezebel, the wife of Ahab was a contemptuous woman, who wanted things to go totally her way. It is vital that a man continues to pray to God for a virtuous woman, so that when the congregation sees a couple, they will surely witness a marriage made in heaven!

Chapter 8

HOLDING ON UNTIL THE END OF THE LINE

Holding on until the end of the line describes a situation of when two people are having problems, but wish to find a remedy before abandoning their marriage. They realize their marriage is at the brink of a break, but still agree to give it another chance before filing for a divorce.

During the effort to preserve their marriage all sort of ideas pass through their minds. For instance, "I can't take anymore from this loser". I've been lonely for so long until I can't hold on any longer. "He or she is just lying to me to prolong this matrimony". Didn't we try this before? Ha, it may or may not work, so I'm going to hang in there to see what happens.

Marriage is like the Children of Israel wondering in the wilderness, a three day journey which lasted up to forty years of traveling. The first three days of a marriage are usually the best ever experienced. However, during the advancement of a marriage, the road can become pretty hectic! That is why a wedding cake should be made smooth and rough at the top, because somewhere along the course of a marriage, there are some rocky roads to journey.

A person's approach to a marriage will largely determine it's out come. A person shouldn't just talk their way into a relationship if they're not ready to walk the walk. A person should approach a relationship with a straight and honest face, and just be themselves. It is obvious that a solid relationship can never survive from false pretenses. The two parties must be straight with each other from the start! Remember what Shakespeare said: "To thine own self be true".

A couple should avoid entering into a relationship like a chameleon. Now, a chameleon is a tropical lizard that has the ability to change colors with its environment; a unique picture of how some marriages operate. Day by day a couple will eventually experience such an occurrence, but should just hold on until the end of the line.

Couples to some extent must exhibit the gift of making some minor changes for the welfare of a marriage. It is necessary for an individual to change his or her coldness, or withdrawnness from one another. Communication is the life line of a relationship. If a person fails to change from being silent to becoming more vocal, or from refraining to embrace to embracing, this can seriously hinder the relationship.

It is important to make the necessary changes if there is to be progress. The only drawback to changes is when it goes against one's advantage to move forward. There are two forms of changes, the positive and the negative. The devil can act in a positive manor for a second, before switching back to his old negative character.

It is easy to make a positive change if a person is willing to make the sacrifice, but if not, then the marriage can become a living hell! Many individuals are advised to throw in the towel when the going gets tough. But throwing in the towel is not always the best way of handling a marriage. Couples should be cautious when receiving advice from outsiders, who may be having worse problems in their own marriages.

We mistakenly heed to the advice of individuals who are experiencing crisis within their own home. They pump our heads with their own solutions, which doesn't always work for the best. Sometimes taking advice can offer a solution or con-fusion. It places a couple in the position to know the difference of how to spit out the bones and eat the meat. Taking advice from some individuals who has profited little and destroyed many marriages. It is best to never jump too quickly on outside advice, without first examining the outcome. Only a couple should determine a final decision. In a metaphoric sense, a couple knows how much they have in their marriage account, or what checks to write or not write.

They are aware of how to hold on until the end of the line until things gets better. They may shed many tears throughout their tribulations, having the understanding that with God and faith, all things are possible, ever holding on until the end of the line.

Couples are like professional boxers who are scheduled for a twelve round match. They train for months before going into the ring. After the first round, they look good, but during the third round their legs appear weary, along with other body fatigues. Now during the six round their legs are nearly gone, and their bodies appears to be exhausted, whereas the fans exhibited a cheer and silence, while some shout to throw in the tile! But a little voice in the head of both components, keep echoing, "Keep brawling, there's some fight left in you. You've gone too far to quit. If you just hold on to the end of the line, help will soon arrive. Your marriage is about to transform from worse to better, if you just hold on to the end of the line".

Chapter 9

UNTIL DEATH DO US PART?

Some couples are so lonely in their marriages, that death really doesn't sound so bad after all. They feel like they have wasted their whole lives dealing with a marriage that has never functioned well. Many felt that their own marriage was in serious trouble, but hung in there, because they loved the idea of just being married, rather than face the experience of a divorce. They kept their spouse for fear of what neighbors and friends would say.

There are dozens of people who are unhappy in their marriages, but will still go through the act that every thing is splendid, until death do them part. Their marriages may have ended decades ago, but they still publicly carried it on as if all was well. Behind closed doors they seldom communicate, sleep in separate bed rooms, and would leave and return home at separate times. They have different friends, bank accounts and even attend different churches.

We hear of these complaints in such manners: "When is he going to become a man, stop chasing women, and handle his responsibility? He's always in the street. When will she start cooking and cleaning up the house? We have no finances because he has too many families outside his own".

In such union we find the husband's wife treated like a poor misused concubine, living in the projects, riding in a beat-up car, while his girl friends are riding in Mercedes, and living in the suburbs. Within such union the husband and wife are impeded from making love to each other, because both are afraid of catching some type of sexually transmittal disease, but regardless, they tolerate each other in spite of such conditions.

The marriage has been over for a long period, but because of their vows unto God, they both will go to their graves as married and lonely.

The couple would rather live in a miserable marriage rather then face a divorce; they dread the thought of lawyers and paper work. They have lived in misery for so long until they have become accustomed to its pain.

Their friends and relatives have encouraged them over and over to leave their marriage, but they found it difficult to escape the echoes of their vows. They would rather live in wretchedness than to separate and attempt to find a new happiness.

Pastors should never take on the responsibility to tell a couple to separate or divorce. The bible speaks of divorce, but what about separation? In some situations separation may be the best answer, giving a person a chance to clear up their heads before executing a divorce. Well, the couple did take a vow, "Until death do us part".

Separation is a condition of robbing Peter and giving to Paul, because most problems increase following a breakup. They become even lonelier, and seek to resolve their loneliness with another companion before a divorce.

A couple in marriages would like to have the perfect marriage, but that's not realistic. They erroneously base a companionship upon the belief of 50/ 50, which in reality is not feasible.

Regardless of how much a spouse may love the other, only God understands the meter of love. A spouse can tell his mate that he loves her about 57% and that she loves him 43%. However, love can never be measured upon a percentage, or determined through the purchase of objects. The definition of love is a complexity, involving the act of reaching out, followed by a return of courtesy. Love is an unpredictable business. It is so strong that when a person hurts, their surroundings often share in the trauma. For example, when a person cries, their mate usually does the same. It is well known that when old couples die, their mates will usually die soon afterward. Now that's a unique example of "Till death do us part".

There was an account of an elder who died, and his wife during the funeral also died. She loved him so much that she couldn't live without him. The family had informed her not to attend the funeral, but she believed that her days were numbered to follow. She wanted to see her husband just one more time, and while viewing the body, she slipped into his arms and died.

Now, if a spouse has experienced so many years of loneliness and unhappiness in a marriage, when their mate dies, they will usually find themselves during the funeral, planning to remarry. Now that's what a lonely heart will do. However, many marriages never last until the death of a spouse.

Another married and lonely situation was the biblical Leah, Rachel and Jacob, whose lives had a similar character to a modern day marriage. Remember Solomon's comments: "... there is no new thing under the sun".

Let us scripturally re-examine the story of Jacob.

Genesis 29

¹Then Jacob went on his journey, and came into the land of the people of the east.

²And he looked, and behold a well in the field, and, lo, there were three flocks of sheep lying by it; for out of that well they watered the flocks: and a great stone was upon the well's mouth.

³And thither were all the flocks gathered: and they rolled the stone from the well's mouth, and watered the sheep, and put the stone again upon the well's mouth in his place.

⁴And Jacob said unto them, My brethren, whence be ye? And they said, Of Haran are we.

⁵And he said unto them, Know ye Laban the son of Nahor? And they said, We know him.

⁶And he said unto them, Is he well? And they said, He is well: and, behold, Rachel his daughter cometh with the sheep.

⁷And he said, Lo, it is yet high day, neither is it time that the cattle should be gathered together: water ye the sheep, and go and feed them.

⁸And they said, We cannot, until all the flocks be gathered together, and till they roll the stone from the well's mouth; then we water the sheep.

⁹And while he yet spake with them, Rachel came with her father's sheep; for she kept them.

¹⁰And it came to pass, when Jacob saw Rachel the daughter of Laban his mother's brother, and the sheep of Laban his mother's brother, that Jacob went near, and rolled the stone from the well's mouth, and watered the flock of Laban his mother's brother.

¹¹And Jacob kissed Rachel, and lifted up his voice, and wept.

¹²And Jacob told Rachel that he was her father's brother, and that he was Rebekah's son: and she ran and told her father.

¹³And it came to pass, when Laban heard the tidings of Jacob his sister's son, that he ran to meet him, and embraced him, and kissed him, and brought him to his house. And he told Laban all these things.

¹⁴And Laban said to him, Surely thou art my bone and my flesh. And he abode with him the space of a month.

¹⁵And Laban said unto Jacob, Because thou art my brother, shouldest thou therefore serve me for nought? tell me, what shall thy wages be?

¹⁶And Laban had two daughters: the name of the elder was Leah, and the name of the younger was Rachel.

¹⁷Leah was tender eyed; but Rachel was beautiful and well favoured.

¹⁸And Jacob loved Rachel; and said, I will serve thee seven years for Rachel thy younger daughter.

¹⁹And Laban said, It is better that I give her to thee, than that I should give her to another man: abide with me.

²⁰And Jacob served seven years for Rachel; and they seemed unto him but a few days, for the love he had to her.

²¹And Jacob said unto Laban, Give me my wife, for my days are fulfilled, that I may go in unto her.

²²And Laban gathered together all the men of the place, and made a feast.

²³And it came to pass in the evening, that he took Leah his daughter, and brought her to him; and he went in unto her.

²⁴And Laban gave unto his daughter Leah Zilpah his maid for an handmaid.

²⁵And it came to pass, that in the morning, behold, it was Leah: and he said to Laban, What is this thou hast done unto me? did not I serve with thee for Rachel? wherefore then hast thou beguiled me?

²⁶And Laban said, It must not be so done in our country, to give the younger before the firstborn.

²⁷Fulfil her week, and we will give thee this also for the service which thou shalt serve with me yet seven other years.

²⁸And Jacob did so, and fulfilled her week: and he gave him Rachel his daughter to wife also.

²⁹And Laban gave to Rachel his daughter Bilhah his handmaid to be her maid.

³⁰And he went in also unto Rachel, and he loved also Rachel more than Leah, and served with him yet seven other years.

³¹And when the LORD saw that Leah was hated, he opened her womb: but Rachel was barren.

³²And Leah conceived, and bare a son, and she called his name Reuben: for she said, Surely the LORD hath looked upon my affliction; now therefore my husband will love me.

³³And she conceived again, and bare a son; and said, Because the LORD hath heard I was hated, he hath therefore given me this son also: and she called his name Simeon.

³⁴And she conceived again, and bare a son; and said, Now this time will my husband be joined unto me, because I have born him three sons: therefore was his name called Levi.

³⁵And she conceived again, and bare a son: and she said, Now will I praise the LORD: therefore she called his name Judah; and left bearing.

Genesis 30

¹And when Rachel saw that she bare Jacob no children, Rachel envied her sister; and said unto Jacob, Give me children, or else I die.

²And Jacob's anger was kindled against Rachel: and he said, Am I in God's stead, who hath withheld from thee the fruit of the womb?

³And she said, Behold my maid Bilhah, go in unto her; and she shall bear upon my knees, that I may also have children by her.

⁴And she gave him Bilhah her handmaid to wife: and Jacob went in unto her.

⁵And Bilhah conceived, and bare Jacob a son.

⁶And Rachel said, God hath judged me, and hath also heard my voice, and hath given me a son: therefore called she his name Dan.

⁷And Bilhah Rachel's maid conceived again, and bare Jacob a second son.

⁸And Rachel said, With great wrestlings have I wrestled with my sister, and I have prevailed: and she called his name Naphtali.

⁹When Leah saw that she had left bearing, she took Zilpah her maid, and gave her Jacob to wife.

¹⁰And Zilpah Leah's maid bare Jacob a son.

¹¹And Leah said, A troop cometh: and she called his name Gad.

¹²And Zilpah Leah's maid bare Jacob a second son.

¹³And Leah said, Happy am I, for the daughters will call me blessed: and she called his name Asher.

¹⁴And Reuben went in the days of wheat harvest, and found mandrakes in the field, and brought them unto his mother Leah. Then Rachel said to Leah, Give me, I pray thee, of thy son's mandrakes.

¹⁵And she said unto her, Is it a small matter that thou hast taken my husband? and wouldest thou take away my son's mandrakes also? And Rachel said, Therefore he shall lie with thee to night for thy son's mandrakes.

¹⁶And Jacob came out of the field in the evening, and Leah went out to meet him, and said, Thou must come in unto me; for surely I have hired thee with my son's mandrakes. And he lay with her that night.

¹⁷And God hearkened unto Leah, and she conceived, and bare Jacob the fifth son.

¹⁸And Leah said, God hath given me my hire, because I have given my maiden to my husband: and she called his name Issachar.

¹⁹And Leah conceived again, and bare Jacob the sixth son.

²⁰And Leah said, God hath endued me with a good dowry; now will my husband dwell with me, because I have born him six sons: and she called his name Zebulun.

²¹And afterwards she bare a daughter, and called her name Dinah.

²²And God remembered Rachel, and God hearkened to her, and opened her womb.

²³And she conceived, and bare a son; and said, God hath taken away my reproach:

²⁴And she called his name Joseph; and said, The LORD shall add to me another son.

²⁵And it came to pass, when Rachel had born Joseph, that Jacob said unto Laban, Send me away, that I may go unto mine own place, and to my country.

²⁶Give me my wives and my children, for whom I have served thee, and let me go: for thou knowest my service which I have done thee.

²⁷And Laban said unto him, I pray thee, if I have found favour in thine eyes, tarry: for I have learned by experience that the LORD hath blessed me for thy sake.

²⁸And he said, Appoint me thy wages, and I will give it.

²⁹And he said unto him, Thou knowest how I have served thee, and how thy cattle was with me.

³⁰For it was little which thou hadst before I came, and it is now increased unto a multitude; and the LORD hath blessed thee since my coming: and now when shall I provide for mine own house also?

³¹And he said, What shall I give thee? And Jacob said, Thou shalt not give me any thing: if thou wilt do this thing for me, I

³²I will pass through all thy flock to day, removing from thence all the speckled and spotted cattle, and all the brown cattle among the sheep, and the spotted and speckled among the goats: and of such shall be my hire.

³³So shall my righteousness answer for me in time to come, when it shall come for my hire before thy face: every one that is not speckled and spotted among the goats, and brown among the sheep, that shall be counted stolen with me.

³⁴And Laban said, Behold, I would it might be according to thy word.

Married and Lonely

³⁵And he removed that day the he goats that were ringstraked and spotted, and all the she goats that were speckled and spotted, and every one that had some white in it, and all the brown among the sheep, and gave them into the hand of his sons.

³⁶And he set three days' journey betwixt himself and Jacob: and Jacob fed the rest of Laban's flocks.

³⁷And Jacob took him rods of green poplar, and of the hazel and chestnut tree; and pilled white strakes in them, and made the white appear which was in the rods.

³⁸And he set the rods which he had pilled before the flocks in the gutters in the watering troughs when the flocks came to drink, that they should conceive when they came to drink.

³⁹And the flocks conceived before the rods, and brought forth cattle ringstraked, speckled, and spotted.

⁴⁰And Jacob did separate the lambs, and set the faces of the flocks toward the ringstraked, and all the brown in the flock of Laban; and he put his own flocks by themselves, and put them not unto Laban's cattle.

⁴¹And it came to pass, whensoever the stronger cattle did conceive, that Jacob laid the rods before the eyes of the cattle in the gutters, that they might conceive among the rods.

⁴²But when the cattle were feeble, he put them not in: so the feebler were Laban's, and the stronger Jacob's.

⁴³And the man increased exceedingly, and had much cattle, and maidservants, and menservants, and camels, and asses.

Before observing the bible's account, let's focus more on today's similar stories.

There is a story of a young man whom after hearing the saga of Leah, Rachel and Jacob, revealed his own story about a young girl that he admired. But before getting involved with this girl he had to first follow the procedure of her aunt, agreeing that he would wait for her. The big surprise is that his friend also fell in love with the same girl. Now, in the process of being watched by the aunt the young girl became pregnant by his friend. His confession is that he still loved the young woman even though he never had a chance to personally be with her.

Once again the bible says, "There's nothing new under the sun." The story of Leah and Jacob is a serious love triangle, because Leah loved Jacob, and Jacob love Rachel. Jacob's willingness to labor for Rachel was side tracked by the tender eye of Leah. He didn't want Leah, but apparently Leah's charm had some positive good toward his acceptance. He didn't like her appearance but was fascinated with her assets. Even though Jacob's first wife was Leah, his mind and heart was centered on Rachel. Now if that's not married and lonely what is it?

Leah was never Jacob's first choice, however being the man he was considerate enough to wait another seven years to be with her sister Rachel.

We should be reminded of the custom of how a father gives up his daughters in foreign nations, and when the groom receives a daughter, he is saying with all do respect "I'm willing to treat your daughter like a queen." Even to this very day some parents select their children's spouse. Can you imagine your mother and father picking your spouse, the person you have to live with for the rest of your life? An individual you know nothing about, but finding yourself saying until death do us part? Poor Jacob, he was a player who got played on. He was a victim of his own game!

There are married and lonely couples out there, who are caught up in a love triangle as was Jacob. The love triangle seems heavenly given at first, but as the years pass, a person will likely work seven more years to acquire the one he or she really loves. A love triangle is like a change of seasons, or Day Light Saving's Time. A person can't reverse the clock of time, like in the fall time goes back an hour, and in spring, up an hour. We're told that time doesn't stand still, and that it can accelerate to the speed of light. Well, a love triangle is just as unpredictable; the stakes are so high with feelings on the line. Just imagine in today's world of having a multiple partnership, trying to observe a sacred vow "Until death do us part".

Some women have the spirit of Leah, knowing that their mate detest them, but have chosen to have children with their man in order to persuade him to favor them; as Leah said: "Now there-fore my husband will love me"(Genesis 29:32). In verse 34 after having more children Leah said, "Now this time will my hus-band be joined unto me, because I have born him three sons". In verse 35, she finely realized who to thank. She said, "Now will I praise the Lord": therefore she called his name Judah.

This type of behavior is largely practiced by younger people, in order to keep their lovers. If a person doesn't love you for whom you are, then it is best to get out of the relationship while you're ahead, because a child can't make another person love their spouse any more than a spouse can explain to a child of why it's okay to leave their mommy or daddy. Some couples are married and lonely because they have applied the wrong techniques to preserve a union. They have erred in their belief by thinking its right to have as many children as possible in order to hold on to a marriage.

The flip side of '"Until death do us part", is when a couple is married and lonely, and can't hold the marriage together before meeting their Maker! There are dozens of stories about couples hating themselves so much until one will kill the other, rather than spend the rest of their lives together.

Is killing someone worth having such guilt over their heads for the rest of their lives? Some people who are married and lonely will never abandon their spouse, simply because of personal health coverage, and other home privileges, benefits that means more to them than the marriage itself.

Maybe the whole world should pay more attention to the popular country singer Kenny Rogers, who once expressed in a song many years ago, ("You have to know when to hold them, know when to fold them, know when to walk away know when to run".)

In some married and lonely situations a person needs to know when and how to vacate (remove one's self from) the premises! Remember, a hero is not necessarily a person who will remain in an unhappy situation, but one who knows when it's over, and then it's over! Realizing that by remaining in an unproductive affair, serves no real purpose; as a Greek warrior once said, "He who runs today is able to fight another day".

Chapter 10

THE BEFORE AND AFTER MARRIAGE

Most married people look at the previous or "Before", and fail to observe or evaluate the "After".

The "Before" can be described as when a person impresses their spouses with favorable sayings such as: "I'll Do all I can to make you happy"; "Your smile brightens my day"; "I love the way you walk and talk"; "Your deodorant and perfume smell like flowers and roses"; "Your scent smells refreshing and brand new"; "My life revolves around you"; The air you breathe brings life unto me"; I see no wrong in you"; "When God created you he broke the mold"; "You're everything a spouse could want and more"; "I love your physical shape and your love is all I need"; "I respect your ideas", etc., etc.

When a person marries another, they marry the "Before", and really don't want the "After," because the "After" has so many mysteries and challenges to sift or filter out. Many couples have gone through the boot camp training experience in their marriages, and find it difficult to declare war upon one another. In the "Before" they were the best of friends, ever reminding the other that their meeting was the best thing that ever happened to them. When people meet each other they commonly see their best sides, which is like a job interview where the two wear their best apparels. Their quick interest in one another caused them to ignore crucial warning signs that should have been instantly questioned closely, before making marital plans.

The "Before" is when couples put their best foot forward to impress the other. Their personal guards are often down because they do not want to stir up any waves in their new relation-ship. The "Before" is really not the true individual, because a straight out honest person will do or say things, which the other party probably wouldn't condone or tolerate during their first date.

Some things that might change after a marriage:

- Around your family
- Hanging out with friends
- Dinner
- Sex
- Personal appearance
- Talking all night on the phone about nothing.
- Getting out of bed, for each other wants (Water, Snack, etc.)
- Leaving the house anytime.
- Splurging
- Friendship
- Support
- Shopping together
- Sports
- House cleaning
- Supporting step children
- Going to church with you
- Compliments
- Gifts (flowers, Jewry, perfumes etc.)
- Going to movies / spending quality time together
- Anniversaries
- Birth days
- Communication
- Spending quality time together

The "Before" is the gamer (Defined as the thrill of the hunt)! A spouse will do things that they usually wouldn't do to attract an individual in order to reel in a catch. But a person can only play a treachery game for so long, where even a child will become tired of such redundancy and come in doors to take a nap. A gamer will change after the hunt is over, and afterward go back to his or her old natural self. The hunter will usually transform back into their real selves after becoming publicly exposed. So if people would be more honest in the early stages of a relationship, it would definitely make marriage more comfortable, or easier to manage. One of the wisest approaches to a courtship is for couples to set down and share some of their hidden agendas, if they wish to secure a harmonious matrimony.

The "After" is what turns a marriage into a tail spin. It is obvious that a couple after so many years would become accustomed to the "Before," which over time will condition them to be pampered. But the "After" comes in like a hurricane or a bad tornado, and before one can see what's going on, they are usually looking right into the eye of a storm; which in all probability will tear up everything in its range.

The "After" is the real marriage! Some women during a courtship would put up with everything their man would do; for instance, spending a lot of time with his parents and other relatives. However, after the marriage vows, those same women will gradually shift their behavior and lay down a different rule. A person's sexual preference is often predicted or anticipated by their mate. However, if either party exhibits any form of deception, the agreement to continue a fruitful sexual encounter may come to a temporary or even a permanent halt.

Many couples go into shock following the "After" marriage. A man will apply untold strategies before a marriage. He will try all types of tricks to get the lady of his dreams, and vice-versa with women who may have other alternatives.

After the woman has yielded herself to her man, she is oftentimes ready to be pampered after an encounter. Both parties can become seriously cunning in their dealings to acquire individual objectives.

During courtship many woman will allow a man to run all the game he chooses, until the marriage takes place. It is after the marriage that many women will use their strategies to redefine things, which most men are not ready for. Women are very smart and practice a lot of patience to make all the right moves. It's like a war game, where men will use all their admonition at once, while women will sit back and think out a strategy to preserve ammo, before advancing a verbal attack.

Men usually go into marriage thinking the marriage is going to remain the same. They believe that most women do not like sports, but before the marriage would go along with the idea of watching sports, and observing nearly every sport channel the man suggests. Nevertheless, following the marriage, things may take a different turn. Neither party should become dismayed, because within every matrimony exists a mutual demonstration, or act of sharing. Both parties must compromise or come to an agreement to partake in the other person's interest, which is difficult but can be managed. They must come to the understanding that dating and marriage are two different life experiences. The things they may have gotten away with while dating, no longer exist in their new marriage. Ha, there are two bosses in a new marriage, but only one head. Now, how can that description become mutually understood?

Marriage is definitely contrary to dating. Some couples will let their spouses know how much they love them, but at the same time, will tell the other how much they rejected many of the other's actions while dating.

It would be wonderful if couples wouldn't give up so easily in their marriages, realizing that they have a lot to accomplish. Many married couples never wanted to go through any form of trial or tribulation! How ironic it is that church people, who teach others how to live, find themselves to have the highest divorce rate. The belief that I am "Holier than thou" should be questioned, or examined among church members. A perfect marriage isn't guaranteed to church participants! A couple who desires a successful marriage must strive to put their best effort into their marriage. The idea that hard work, tears, and disappointment in a union aren't an option isn't a useful one. Let's face it, a marriage is not as simple as blinking one's eye. It takes 99% of perspiration (work), and 1% of aspiration (dream or desire). It's like the phrase; True respect is earned and not given. It's like the art of cooking, which may take a while to develop. However, many couples who are looking for a quick fix, or a short lived dream, may foolishly avoid the principal of waiting, by utilizing the expedience of a 'microwave fix'. After realizing a bad taste in their relationship, because of their careless rushing, has caused many to trash the marriage before seeking help.

Entering into a marriage with the feeling that everything is wonder-fully alright, without acknowledging that a marriage may experience some crises, is fatal! The best part of a marriage is when couples can look back over the years, and learn from their experiences.

Lots of individuals in their marriages look for any excuse to run from or evade critical issues. There are many of our leaders in power who may have been married three, four, or even five times. How can a society teach others on how to preserve a marriage when its own counsels have practiced the very opposite of what they profess to teach?

Our institutions should instruct couples that their "After" is not as bad as seems; Life can become better from hard work and prayers. A road may become rough, but if a couple continues to drive forward with a positive view, then that same road will become smoother.

Remember, this topic is about the "Before and After", and this book is not written to influence any persons to leave, separate, or divorce from their spouse. All marriages are not the same, and should be studied from different perspectives.

Is it wise to recommend a troubled marriage to see a professional counselor, with accredited degrees, not knowing if the counsel is a fly by night "know it all" should someone else other than God administer a couple's crises?

It is known that the United States military are always training and playing war games for battle; ever strengthening their mental ability for war. But no matter how much a person pre-pares for war, every war is an unpredictable affair. Yet, playing war games and actually being in a real war happens to be two different experiences. The benefit of playing war games is that a person can smilingly end the game without suffering any physical injuries; not likely in a real war! Even though the experience of a painful marriage may appear to have equal affects.

Chapter 11

FROM A MARRIAGE VOWS TO A FINANCIAL TRANSACTION?

De 23:21

When thou shalt **vow** a **vow** unto the LORD thy God, thou shalt not slack to pay it: for the LORD thy God will surely require it of thee; and it would be sin in thee.

There's a major difference between a marriage vow and a financial transaction. In a marriage it takes a triangle method to make it work, which is communication, sex and finance. If one of these three ingredients is missing in matrimony then the marriage is likely to eat away. A marriage definitely needs communication, because without this vital virtue both parties will likely end up discussing their secrets to someone else. It's not wise for a couple to openly discuss their personnel affairs with another close associate of the opposite sex. It has been known that a close associate whom a person share their secrets with, can often come between a marriage and destroy it. There are couples who have put their business into the hands of the opposite sex, and found themselves pursuing a divorce, in hopes of marrying the same person they confided in. It should be widely understood that if a person divorces their mate for another associate, then that divorcee will likely repeat the process with their new mate.

A marriage vow is not a promise, because a promise can be broken or changed to fit the needs of a situation. A person might not perceive a vow to be serious, but it involves telling God that he or she will fulfill the vow made to Him by any means necessary.

If a person knows without a shadow of a doubt, that they can't carry out a vow, then they shouldn't commit to it. If a person comes to the table with several prenuptial agreements involving marriage, then it is crystal-clear that the marriage might not work; a way of saying I am protecting myself. A prenuptial agreement is a declaration of saying "I really don't trust you the way I should". I must trust my own instincts, having nothing against you, even though I am given you my last name, you will not get all of my assets if this union doesn't work".

A marriage is much more than saying "I presently love you and maybe later". What about when a person finds out that the food they're eating at their mate's home doesn't belong to the spouse but from a little moms and pops kitchen. What if they find out that the desert, being that good old apple pie was from the bakery down the street, along with the cloths he or she wore to impress the other was borrowed from a relative. Also, knowing that the idea of purchasing a gift is suggested from a book called, How to Catch a Spouse101. Last but not least, the verbal expression of love spoken from their own lips was copied from soap operas or movies. Realizing that the tactics the person used to lure their love interest was not of themselves, but merely borrowed lines.

When a person runs out of other people's maneuvers or games to prepare for their own wedding, it may force that person to revert to their natural selves. Please realize that the devil is as a snake, and can bend the truth only so far. So when he strikes he may entice many to perform outside of their normal behavior. In a marriage it is awfully hard to predict a situation.

A lot of couples have confessed to have never noticed anything out of order while they were dating. It isn't what they didn't see, but didn't want to see, which turned their marital affair in such a lonely and agitated state.

Married and Lonely

A marriage can have its difficulties, because it's when two individuals with a totally different backgrounds, raised in separate times with distinct cultural values. Just imagine how two people who want to share a life together had to first find mutual ground in order to effectively intercommunicate. One key to a marriage is hard work with a clear open communication; a person must work at it twenty four-seven. It comes with a lot of overtime, and is certainly not a favorable job for a lazy person.

All marriages go through fazes. Some are for better and some are for worst; it's an up and down mountain-top and valley-low experience. It's all about how much time a person desires to put into their marriage to bring it up to satisfaction.

In a marriage a person must take the good, the bad as well as the ugly; an experience which many will never understand, until things change for the better.

When a couple has done all they can to make a marriage work, and neither want to remove their wedding rings and persue a divorce, then once again the couples are going through a stage of married and lonely. Such situations have lead many mates to seek other parties to satisfy their ultimate. How misfortunate, that when there were once two parties, now there's four! How sad that couples allow such to occur, having no more respect for the other than maintaining financial security.

Once a marriage has become a financial money agreement, both parties depend upon each other's income to survive in life.

They need one another's support, desiring the finest things in life where upon a single income would never work. They refuse to let the other go because of the material things they may lose, such as a joint bank account, which looks better on paper, than having a single account with the other party as co-signer. Every-thing they enact is like a chess game, knowing that someone has to lose. Now, the marriage has become like a bargaining affair, for as: "You do something for me and I'll do the same for you". What a game to play, thinking of themselves as married and lonely and feeling that everyone else has a perfect marriage except for them; not knowing that someone down the street has it four time worse than them.

A marriage centered on a financial transaction is nothing more than having a "room mate" with a piece of paper. This is a situation where a person values money over matrimony. Sometimes when the money gets low, one party in the marriage can end up in the hands of someone wealthier.

Chapter 12

YOU GET WHAT YOU PAY FOR

Let it be widely acknowledged that a person can fowl-up a good relationship by mistakenly thinking that they can win the heart of a person by sizing them up; failing to grasp that a relationship requires much more than an individual's opinion, based on inadequate guessing.

If a person learns to go into a relationship with some what a 50/50 concept; realizing that there may be two bosses in a family, but only one head to lead the family, they will likely establish a firm foundation for family development. A family structure should offer equal treatment, for example, let the husband pay for a meal one day, and allow other capable family members to pick-up the tab on another occasion. What other example would exhibit a greater way of sharing responsibility?

Some people are married and lonely because they think the gifts of a marriage are free; this is not so. There is a price to pay for every element of life. Remember, Salvation was never free because Jesus paid a price for us all.

It's amazing to see young men buying their girl friends candy, toys, rings, necklaces, watches and so on. And then say, "I love you," and can't even spell the word love, or know the slightest meaning of love. Ironically, young men at an early age believe if he buys a young woman a gift then he owns her, and when the relationship ends the young man wants all the candy, toys, rings, and necklaces or watches to be returned. He even goes as far as spearing the young girl's name. How dreadful that a once beautiful friendship has now turned into a badly behaved war. A once close relationship now has been turned into an adversarial description.

A person's childhood past never ends by leaving the parent's home, or his or her state. That's just not how it's defined! One's past is evaluated or incorporated into every second whom passes during ounce's life.

A young person's behavior toward the opposite sex is largely based on his or her past. A young man may feel that after all of the merchandise, material, or monies that he has invested into his love affair in some way buys her, but denies her the power of choice to decide her own destiny.

A young person's past can surely shape their adult behavior. They may begin a friendship by sending their intended flowers and rings, and sometimes gifts that the receiver normally couldn't afford. In the process of such behavior, the buyer must carefully re-examine his approach, by acknowledging that his mate has the freedom to determine her own direction after receiving such gifts. Buyers must understand that their purchase doesn't guarantee them the right to own that mate.

Many individuals can remember their parent's comment: "Money can't buy you love". Therefore, in the midst of many marriages a person will only get what they have paid for. If he or she pays to have a shopping buddy, a gold digger or a hustler, then again they have only gotten what they have paid for. When a needy person's money is low and the bills are due, this scenario can certainly produce some real actors and actresses to step forward on the stage to play some real parts. The giver must be careful that he or she is not killed off the scene like other movie performers. The question is frequently asked how a leading lady or man can be killed off of an episode so soon in the best part of the movie. Well, the simple answer is obvious; the buyer never was the main star from the beginning.

A buyer may go through some lonely moments not feeling as needed as they previously did, realizing that his or her overture toward catching the eye of a mate wasn't the wisest approach. If so, then money wouldn't always be a primary issue in keeping the relationship workable. Yet, most people who love things and money will still have the power to purchase most things in life. What a strategy; to love things and use people, instead of exercising the opposite.

Some individuals are very glad to have met their spouses, because they never expected to receive special favors in their courtship. They are down-right happy because their mates have seriously centered their interest toward them, without first offering them physical gifts. They neither had to go outside their abilities to impress the other! For a reminder, "What you see is what you get". Their mates saw great potential in them which they themselves couldn't observe. Both individuals show the deepness inner regards for each other, and not the surface stuff that could wash so quickly away when trials and tribulations occur.

Parents should teach their children this crucial knowledge at an early age. Informing their children, especially their daughters not to accept money or merchandise from anyone before acquiring parent consent. The young daughter must be informed that there is nothing that a young man should buy her that her own parents couldn't buy. Children need to know that money is an essential, but not the main source of their lives. Some untaught children are selling drugs or even their bodies for money. This is an act that will certainly bring nothing but misery and destruction!

Parents should teach their young men not to buy girls gifts in order to lure them, and if they have already done so, then they should immediately stop; without requesting the return of the gifts. The young men must be reminded that even though it's wrong to buy little girls gifts, that all gifts are a token of love, and should not be offered to acquire a personal privilege.

Parents should also encourage their children to improve their reading and writing skills. The young men in particular should be often briefed on how to be a gentleman, for example, how to open a door for women. They should be reminded of how other great men have served the Lord throughout their lives, based upon action instead of merely lip service.

Chapter 13

=========

GREAT EXPECTATION

It is not unusual for most people to look for the best things in life. A great expectation of one's marriage simply means a person is seeking something bigger than life itself. Great expectation also means that a person is not looking for a loser, failure or just a nobody. Some individuals might remember this about their spouse because of a present experience associated with the "Married and lonely" situation, which in the beginning wasn't so, simply because the only thing they detected about their mate was genuinely perfect. There is absolutely nothing wrong with expecting the best from a spouse, but it shouldn't be to the point of where a person should throw away everything just because of an untimely development in a marriage. If a person's spouse worked at a fast food restaurant before marrying her, then he shouldn't expect a quick change within the first year of their marriage. In reality the change may never occur! However, that doesn't give the spouse the okay to abuse his or her mate, but to treat that person as if they're the owner of the company that they work for! Great expectation is not all bad, nor all good, because sometimes a person may set their mate on a higher social pedestal than what is called for. Yes, a person may expect too much from their mate than what is necessarily required. The union should be centered on the total concern of both individuals, not just one member.

It must feel great to tell someone that they themselves or their spouse is somebody special. The military spouses are good at such deeds. They are so quick to say "My spouse is a Captain, or my mate is in charge of many service personnel".

It is great to say:

- We own a big house.
- My family is well off.
- My spouse's job pays over six figures a year.
- We have a pure bred family dog.
- We can take family vacations any time during the year.
- We own European cars.
- We have a large bank account.
- We have a trusting relationship.
- I have great sex with my spouse often.
- We have great communication.
- I have a blessed family.
- My spouse has advanced college degrees.
- My spouse has advanced college degree

Marriage is not about the subject of Salvation. But it takes the anointing of God to preserve all marriages. Salvation makes marriages easier after both parties have repented, and received the baptism in the name of Jesus, and filled with the Holy Ghost.

Saved married couples should love Jesus and every word that comes from Him, because the Lord is still speaking clearer than ever before! Does the world recognize His voice? If a person says that he or she acknowledges the word of Jesus, then their next step should be to reminisce on what messages Jesus spoke to them before walking down the isle. How can a person look for great expectation when God was never the center of their marriage? If Christ is not the nucleus of a couple's marriage, then that marriage is really not anointed, but can only be rescued by allowing God to enter.

Once again all marriages will go through some form of disturbance. A person before marrying should have observed what kind of individual their spouse wouldn't or couldn't be. Some saw more potential in their spouse than they could see in themselves. The funny thing about this is that they become shocked when all the flaws come out. Many couples were so overwhelmed by lust until they just avoid major indications of a future break-up. Love is permanent, but lust is only temporary. That's why so many couples end up married and lonely.

Many couples end up married and lonely because they are missing some ingredient from the table of love, which is certainly powerful in unification. The younger person's view of great expectation in a marriage is predominantly based upon sex and lust. But what is going to happen when that beautiful body starts to wear down and loses its shape? Why do men see a marriage different from a woman's perspective? For example, a man who has moved into a starter home will become content for an indefinite period of time, but on the other hand most women won't until they receive their dream home. An individual's expectation has a lot to do with his or her outlook in life. Now some of their goals have exceeded their spouse's abilities, which often bring about humiliation in a marriage, especially if there's a lack of negotiation. Spouses shouldn't become upset when one fails to see eye to eye on certain issues, because one spouse may define a glass as half full, while the other, half empty, yet the same glass but just a different point of view.

An individual's conception of a great expectation should be centered upon the welfare of both parties' abilities to find a common ground, and work as a team regardless of the obstacles. They should pray and fast that the Lord will guide their ambitions into a positive outcome.

Do research on these Scripture:

1. Ephesians 5:23
2. Ephesians 5:31, 32
3. Ephesians 5:25, 26, 28

People are married and lonely for various reasons. But one is centered around the disobedience of God. The Scriptures comment on the husband loving the wife and the wife submitting to her husband. The Lord already understands the differences between a man and a woman which He created. It's hard for some men to show true love, as it is for some woman to show true submission. Most men, who have fought in battles or wars, have a natural instinct to be on the alert for future disruptions.

The most common Greek terms for love:
Again the prime key word for a men and woman is love. And there are different words used for love.

   a. Eros (attraction, sexual love)
   b. Philia (friendship, love)
   c. Agape (love, charity)
   d. Storge (natural affection)

What is love?
A clarification must be stressed regarding the context in which *agape* is engaged in this epistle, from the suffrage beard on the life of the apostles. A magnitude of members of the Corinthian church had been blessed to practice certain supernatural gifts (the gift of healing, speaking in a foreign language, translating a foreign tongue, etc).

Several of these Corinthian Christians, nevertheless, were abusing their spiritual constitutional rights by exercising, or foretelling signs based upon their own vanities, rather than to observe the spiritual practice of their ancestors, whom once walked with God. For example, sometimes there would be several verbal presentations simultaneously, creating an atmosphere of confusion. That was hardly conducive to learning.

In calculation, the apostle noted that the point in time was approaching when certain gifts would be detached from the church's possession. When the revelatory process was completed (with the finished product of the New Testament), the gifts would come to a close (1 Cor. 13:8ff). The discussion of "love" thus serves a twofold function.

1. It seeks to control selfish abuses of spiritual gifts;
2. Love's abiding natural is similarity with the temporal Character of miraculous gifts.

The poise of this debate will enable a person to expound upon the value of agape-love, as described in this perspective. Great expectation is when a person sees love being use in its rightful role.

Love Is Long-suffering (backwards means suffers long).
In the New Testament it has to do with how one ought to respond to abuse. Love patiently waits and attempts to advance over one's adversities.

In a world which is saturated with cruelty, a kind temperament is a refreshing breeze! There are a lot of women who would trade their handsome cruel husbands for a benevolent one, because kindness would certainly heal the plague of family abuse. More kindness among brothers in the Lord would eliminate much of today's church confusion. The Scriptures command that we be kind to one another (Eph. 4:32).

The bible says, "Let another man praise you, and not your own mouth". Now what is a braggart? There are several other questions that should be asked first. Is authentic love selfless, since it seeks to exalt the virtues of other? Now, love has words of encouragement for the loneliness, downtrodden, and others who deserve and need uplifting. Nevertheless, is it right for some individuals to boast or encourage themselves on?

The unique language here denotes one who is inflated with a sense of personal pride. Arrogance is an unreasonable self-encourager, generally accompanied by impudence and ill-mannered treatment of others. It sometimes deceives the heart and hardens the mind, whereas the out come can be destructive.

The Greek term here literally suggests the notion of being "without form." It encompasses all sorts of wickedness, horrendous manners, and brutal rudeness. Love doesn't deliberately seek out to be offensive.

How many people take pride in their ability to love others? The Christian's vocabulary should be characterized by such terminology as, "No, you're first", "Please", "Thank you", "How can I help you?" etc. Love operates with a contentious politeness, where the terms gentleman and lady are often expressed!

Love seeks not its own means or chases its own interests; love isn't woeful-selfish. It has been said that there are two kinds of people, those who are constantly thinking about their rights, and those who concentrates on their personally responsibilities.

Many individuals who are protective concerning their own rights, believes others should fend for themselves. After all, it's a dog-eat-dog jungle out there, from whence came the origin of a fang-and-claw philosophy.

By way of consider the sacrificial example of the Son of God. Love nurses the mind and hearts of all whom request to serve the Almighty.

Love doesn't have a very small fuse; it doesn't wonder with a chip on its shoulder. Some individuals are cocked and loaded to explode, or go to war. Their day is ruined if someone doesn't provide the opportunity for them to share a piece of their mind. Authentic love will do anything possible to avoid combat. If a quarrel occurs concerning truth, then so be it; but one should not live in the objective having a mind frame of vengeance!

This descriptive doesn't indicate that love ignores evil. Such belief would disagree with numerous passages in the bible. There are periods when evil must be exposed, rebuked, and closely controlled. The Greek word for "account" is taken from *logizomai*, a commercial expression which suggests writing as a transaction in the record, so as not to overlook it. Love doesn't maintain a score, for example; "Three times this month he has neglected to speak to me". The one who says, "I must forgive you, but I'll never forget what you did." Such comments have miserably failed the test of "agape", since love doesn't harbor bitterness, nor does it plot vengeance.

Love doesn't rejoice in unrighteousness, but solely in truth. Since love always seeks the good of others, it can by no means rejoice when evil prevails. When a brother falls, even an obnoxious one, a person shouldn't embrace secret thoughts of satisfaction. Rejoicing in moral wickedness is in opposition to Salvation and biblical principals, and doesn't have the humanity welfare at heart. For example, individuals who triumph in parades for "gay privileges," or who cheerfully commemorate the liberalization of abortion laws, have utterly no perception of what real love is about; lacking to acknowledge that love can never separate itself from objective truth.

Love supports or uplifts those who are in need of the Father and Son. Jesus was constantly in danger with numerous Jewish critics, because of His support for the downtrodden.

Furthermore, one who operates out of love will look after and often go slow toward exposing the mistakes of others. Barclay says: "Love would far rather set about quietly mending things than publicly displaying and rebuking them". Of course there may be a time to openly expose a wrong, and as Solomon said: "To every thing there is a season and time to every purpose under the heaven".

This comment doesn't mean that love is easy to fool, because an error is both wrong and hazardous. Rather, the apostle has something else in mind. The sense of the verb *pisteuo* (believes) here is probably that of trusting (Phillips). The word can surely have that meaning, which seems to be applied here. Love will always give the benefit of the doubt. When people hear a distasteful account concerning another fellow Christian, should he hesitate to believe such story? In these times since an error is so rampant in most churches, should a person be hesitant and re-examine the incident before taking sides? Should a person go all out toward giving the benefit of doubt before judging another fellow saint?

Even during the challenging of one's faith, love continues to flourish; Agape demonstrates its strengths which heal all things; it is deeper than human expression! If men can love their wives with such an awesome impact, then the bible wouldn't have to pamper, on how to love.

The Greek word for submission is "hypotasso" or "hypotage".

These words apply to persons who are subjected or subordinates to anything or someone, whether for a good or for bad.

Wife to submit:

Main Entry: **submit**
Function: *verb*

Inflected Forms: **submitted**; **submitting** transitive verb **1** : to yield or subject to control or authority <to *submit* himself to the jurisdiction of the tribal court **2 a** : to present or propose to another for review, consideration, or decision; *specifically* : to commit to a trier of fact or law for decision after the close of trial or argument <the trial court could properly *submit* both counts to the jury —Rorie Sherman> **b** : to deliver formally **3**: to put forward as an opinion or contention intransitive verb **1** : to yield oneself <parties to a contract may agree in advance to *submit* to the jurisdiction of a given court **2** : to defer to or consent to abide by the opinion of another

Submit
v 1: refer for judgment or consideration; "She submitted a proposal to the agency" [syn: subject] 2: put before; "I submit to you that the accused is guilty" [syn: state, put forward, posit] 3: yield to the control of another 4: hand over formally [syn: present] 5: refer to another person for decision or judgment; "She likes to relegate difficult questions to her colleagues" [syn: relegate, pass on] 6: submit or yield to another's wish or opinion; "The government bowed to the military pressure" [syn: bow, defer, accede, give in] 7: accept or undergo, often unwillingly; "We took a pay cut" [syn: take, undergo] 8: make an application as for a job or funding; "We put in a grant to the NSF" [syn: put in] 9: make over as a return; "They had to render the estate" 10: accept as inevitable; "He resigned himself to his fate".

Let it be widely acknowledged that the word "submit" doesn't take an affect after saying "I do", or that a person has purchased me as a new slave. Now, for a quick glimpse of a marriage, involving a person whose experiencing a "Marriage and lonely" situation, may look for any opportunity to run away. A person can become so battered within a relationship that they rather become mauled by blood hound thirsty dogs, then to live in a hellish marriage.... Prayers are constantly offered for the battered and abused. Remembering such comments as: "I hope she make it out of that abusive relationship before she's killed".

One thing that happens in so many relationships is that people enter their marriages with an expectation, greater than what he or she is capable of fulfilling. For instance, if a spouse knew that their mate has never experienced the use of power tools before entering the marriage, then why would the spouse expect her mate to build a house from ground-up? If a man knew his wife couldn't cook before their matrimony, then why should he become horrified about her burning his food?

At certain stages of a marriage spouses craves to be like other couples, failing to realize that every marriage is as different as a person's finger print; that no marriage can work effectively by comparing it to another. Any marriage can be foolishly imagined to be a duplicate of another, but in reality it's totally impossible.

Great expectation is when a person believes another person's achievements are greater than theirs are. Such form of thinking is merely a platform for failure.

Chapter 14

GROW UP

Imagine going back down old memory lane and reminiscing, a segment of when we were children. Naturally we all were children, weren't we? Well let's move onward in regarding our parents who could have had nine or more children. Every one of her children having different personalities, and character. Some as being loud, quiet, selfish, givers, takers, playful, introverts, extroverts, leaders, followers, timid, serious, negative, or positive and so on.

Our childhood is really our whole makeup, some for the best and some for the worst. Our childhood is who we revert back to in life, and in marriage. Many children couldn't wait to grow up. They wanted every conceivable object from a car to heaven knows what. We couldn't wait to move from among our parents to go to clubs and own our homes. But the closer we got to graduating from high school and taking on certain responsibilities, reality started kicking in to what life was about, and it wasn't a pretty picture. Within our homes existed over nine or more children, whom were different in all walks of life; As infants we were born in sin and shaped in iniquity, This is the baggage we carried with us as we left home. Look at our lives now; although we're all grown up, we still have our childhood roots. We can remember as early adolescents receiving an allowance from our parents. Many of us with our big dreams even opened up bank accounts from monies we earned from local jobs such as mowing lawns, waiting or bussing tables, bell hops and being car washers. Many of us had good business sense and were pretty good applying our monies to purchase minor essentials as school materials, future college funds, attending movies, helping the family to buy cornflakes, candy, snowballs, toys, barber shop and beautician fees, bus fare, etc. Our little efforts definitely kept many of us busy and gained a big smile of gratitude from our parents. Many of the young males were taught to never hit or lay hands on any women. Being constantly reminded such an act was totally unacceptable. We all can remember how our moms kept the house real nice and neat, and our dads daily going to work, painting our homes, working on the family automobiles, playing sports and laying the golden rules. Most of us were great thinkers, ever contemplating on the most important aspects of life, and how, when and where our future would lie. Most of us while going through grade school, middle school and high school were thrilled to make the acquaintance of the opposite sex, but they were different in so many ways. We just couldn't avoid noticing how we grew larger and taller in a short period of time. How memorable it is if that young person in grade school was: loud, quiet, slow, expedient, made good or bad grades, were boasters, bullies, liars, thieves, cheaters, fakers, hooky-players, God-lovers, God-haters, leaders, cry-babies, cold-footed, daring, cowards, athletes, business-minded, lazy, drinkers, smokers, etc. Modernly we are still the same as we were when younger, with the exception of the body growth changes.

Let's go back a little farther in life. Remember those children who grew up wanting to do everything on their own; they want to learn how to crawl and walk on their own, having a favorite saying, "I can do it by myself".

Then we have the selfish children, everything was good as long as everything was going their way. As long as they were playing a sport they liked, then all was well. Conversely, they would take their ball and run, saying, "If I can't play with my ball then I won't play the game at all and I will not stay". Now, that is a true characteristic of a marriage with some people.

As many of us visit our families throughout the state, we might run across an old friend and strike-up a conversation about our childhood. How surprising to the eye to see that many are in adult bodies.

Some of us still get angry and may take our ball and run after noticing an adult with a child-like mentality. Those individuals are adults with large families, who have bought cars and homes. But still act odd by throwing temper tantrums; actually having "fits" when they don't get their way! It is amazing how a person grows-up and how they behave everyday in their adult life; some behaviors are honorable and some bad.

Let's observe the birth order of children by selecting the number six for instance: Out of Six children what number was your spouse? Was she the first child, a girl who was more mature and helped to raised the others children? Was he the second child, a boy and spoiled by mom; the first son who tended not to work as hard? Was he the third child, a boy who just wanted to be accepted? Was the forth child, close in age to the third child; they had a lot in common, feeling they were left out, or forgotten? Was he or she the fifth child, spoiled by the parents who after having so many children, choose to lay all the blame on the older four. Did the sixth child have a lot in common with the fifth child, because they "got away" with everything? Now the big question becomes, after you chose to get married, in what order was your spouse born? Was he or she the only child and very spoiled? Out of a family of all the girls was he the only male child? In the long run these questions can have a negative or a positive impact on your family.

All children go through different stages in life; prenatal, infancy, toddler, preschool, puberty and adolescence. Some parents prevent their children from escaping these stages in order to keep them as children. Do you know of any families where the adult children all still living at home? Not because of finances but because of the parents refusal to let their children go in order to enhance their own lives.

Some people are married and lonely because in the beginning of courtship they thought they were marrying an adult, and not a child inside of an adult's body. Just because a man has hair on his face and smells like a man doesn't make him a man. This is also true about a woman, wearing make-up and a bra doesn't make her a woman.

After a person has been married for a while and gotten to know their spouse a little better, they may find that they were unequally yoked in several critical areas. This description is not based solely upon whether couples are Christians or non-Christians, because it is well known, where some marriages are not based around the Christian faith, but have survived until death do them part. But lets get back to the main issue, most couples face mental issues within their marriages. While you are making an adult decision your spouse's mind is out on recess; playing and having fun! They're stuck in a childhood stage, a recessive behavior that only God-Almighty can find a care for, which some would even fight Him to remain in such condition! To change them would be like pulling teeth from the mouth of a crocodile or a lion. Facing reality is a mean business! It's like a college student who after attending her four-years finds herself jobless for the rest of her life.

 We look at life through various stages. People change at certain age and stages of life. The world expects people to behave according their age. Our dress style is an expression of that! What would a person think when seeing an eighty-five year old woman wearing a tight short shirt with her naval showing bearing a ring? What would a person think when observing a forty nine year old man wearing a big gold chain, on a skate board, wearing no shirt while hanging around teenagers? Let's face it, at certain ages your dress code changes when wisdom sets in.

 People look at others in so many different ways, because they're just judgmental by nature. Sometimes they're correct in their judgments while other times they're totally off center. So many of us should ask the big question of how was our judgment. Were we on target or did we miss the mark? Now, since we're married and going through the test of time, are we ourselves facing a "Married and Lonely" experience? In the beginning of our dating we imagined an adult, but farther into the marriage we detected only a child seeking another parent; always insidious or playing games. They avoid responsibilities and still ask their original parents of how to live. Now we're frustrated because we're in a whirlwind relationship, where the marriage ceases to grow, because one party is incapable of mentally facing reality!

Chapter 15

FOR HUSBAND EXCLUSIVE

Let us send a shout-out to all men. Give yourselves a standing ovation, and let every woman know that all men are not dogs. Some women have picked the wrong men to be in her lives, and unfortunately have blamed all men for a few misfits. A man is the king, priest and prophet of his home, who understands that he should obey all orders from God. Sometimes we may get slightly off tract in some areas of our lives. But regardless, still having the strength to say, "We've made an error and let's fix it" (It wasn't the first nor will it be the last, since humans are subject to make errors). It would be a great benefit if women would understand that all men, especially young men. We have seriously undergone a Spiritual, mental and physical attack from Satan.

To exhibit courage and honor in our families, men were taught not to cry during their tribulations, but to stand tall and suck it up! We were taught to fight, protect and defend our values. But as sad as it may sound, for centuries we were deprived of freedom of religion, assembly, the press and speech. Let's be factual, all of us were not taught about the birds and the bees, etc.! We were instructed not to show emotion, or feelings, nor schooled in areas of romance, intimacy and communication. One comment we can clearly remember while growing up is: "I'm a man". We didn't know how to prepare to get a job, or rehearse for an interview, even though it was verbally drilled in us to be manly. Some of us were never schooled to open doors for women or to sit a girl in her seat and slide her chair to the table. We were never taught that it is inappropriate to blow our horns when visiting a young lady's home. We were never instructed to get out of our cars, and introduce ourselves to the girl's parents instead of blowing the horn! Ladies it's hard being a man when most of our homes are ruled by women. But with God's blessings we are more than a person could hope to be. I apologize for what women can't understand, but as long as I realize what God see's in me, then I'm on the right path with Him.

Throughout our childhood, we were never informed of what we needed in life, probably because most males that we looked up to had the same problems, which were unlearned behaviors.

Now as adults, we have become husbands and everything that we've learned as children is about to unfold. I feel like I'm fresh out of boot camp, having been trained too fast and not quite ready to move to the real part of life. How interesting, because on my wedding day while I was heading to the alter and waiting for my bride; all of a sudden reality hit, and I wondered what I was doing standing before so many people. Thinking that there was one thing that my future bride didn't realize, and that was that I didn't have a clue of what was involved in making a marriage work. From the beginning of planning the wedding to the final stage of saying "I do", the biggest question was, "What comes next?"

Now after a few weeks of being married with an overload of various responsibilities, a loud horn went off in my head saying, "What in the world has just happened here?" The girl I love has invented a set of new rules out of the clear blue. Certainly she let me know that there is a new sheriff in town. Softly and quietly reminding me that my old female associates were no longer needed, and that she was my best friend forever! Well, every man loves a strong woman, but she had to be reminded that she was drawing too fast from the hip, before I could even justify my legal standing. A man learns as he goes through the process of marriage that he is usually guilty of something before an act is even committed!

To make things even worse he's guilty upon mere speculation until proven innocent, an injustice that has followed him all the way to the penitentiary, which only a DNA test can exonerate him! Now, the only divine manual a couple has to guide their marriage is the word of God. So once again please forgive us men when making a mistake, which just doesn't add up to any sensible means. A wife, who stands at the crossroads of a marriage, can either make her husband or break him. Many wives or Christian women who believe in the power of prayer should seriously encourage their husbands to keep their eyes on the prize, by attending church, college, City Hall and PTA meetings, and many other important social functions. A wife's encouragement is the glue or fabric in a family structure. When a man has an understanding wife he has a magnificent jewel of a person in his corner. Many nagging women have actually driven their men away from home. Remember what Proverbs 21:9 says about a nagging woman: "It is better to dwell in the wilderness, than with a contentious and an angry woman".

There are a lot of married and lonely men in our society, who are just coasting through life, pretending that everything is alright. They will fabricate the truth to keep harmony in their homes, for instance; if their oversized wives ask them about their weight, some husbands will give a big compliment instead of criticizing them for eating too much. Some men are walking a very thin line with their wives, knowing that they're in hot water if they say anything inappropriate.

Now, when it comes to making love it's like playing a game of jack and ball and jump-rope. I remember when I was younger watching young girls playing Double Dutch. The rope was moving so fast with two ropes moving at the same time, until it made my head swim. Some men are married and lonely because they don't know when to jump in, and jump out, if you know what I mean! One way of frustrating and killing the spirit of a man is to deprive him of his intimate rights. Nevertheless, many men within their marriages are outside the ropes rocking back and forward waiting to be allowed to reenter.

The man is screaming saying, "How can a woman say a man wants sex all the time, when the lord has given her body a week of rest for one week out of the month". The man regularly hears the woman complaining about their head hurting, or "I'm too tired".

Some women have forced some men into cheating, which by no means justify a man's behavior. Some women are so "Holier than thou," that they fail to recognize that a man loves Jesus just as much as they, and that there is a time and a place for everything. Hebrew 13:4 says: "Marriage *is* honorable in all, and the bed undefiled: but whoremonger and adulterers God will judge".

The wives shouldn't force their husband to seek extra marital affairs by denying him matrimonial rights. Some men, and not all, are looking for any excuse to cheat on their spouse. So it's not wise for wives to give their husbands a reason to commit such ill-virtuous acts, by rejecting them certain privileges. A man being turned down by his wife time after time can generate frustration and resentment. A rejection can rip down a man's self-esteem, because in his eyes he's a Lion-King. But if a man continues to be rejected, he is surely a victim of "Married and Lonely", since he has no one to express his feelings to. Women have a greater network than men.

They will communicate with friends concerning any or everything, whereas a man will hold things inside until it reaches a boiling point, knowing that their wives are not up to granting them their rights. Some men are saying, "If I go to my wife to make love to her, what if I desired her every night? "Will she be happy instead of being disappointed"? Let's be fair about it, women are not always happy about having sex once a week, certainly not every night. So when a man goes outside his home and commits adultery, it is obvious that the whole marriage suffers. Actually both parties have sinned by undercutting or going overboard. The wife by holding back and the husband by giving in, which is of the greater sins?

Even though husbands and wives have their difficulties there are no justifiers of why either party should put their hands on the other. How can either spouse strike the other if they are actually in love, then how can love destroy love? If a person treats their spouse like an animal, then they are subjected to be "Married and lonely" until the marriage improves. Some dogs are treated better than some spouses.

A man wants his wife to know that he can be romantic other than just sleeping with her. Most women feel it doesn't take very much to excite them. So here are some tips given to men from women.

Romance tips:

- ♥ A simple card
- ♥ Give flowers for no reason at all.
- ♥ I love you phone calls.
- ♥ A tender touch not leading to sex.
- ♥ Make love on a beach.
- ♥ Plan a secret lunch date.
- ♥ Play a romantic CD.
- ♥ Give a sexy gift.
- ♥ Send love notes.
- ♥ Give each other hot oil massages.
- ♥ Take a bubble bath together.
- ♥ Plan a his and her day at the spa.
- ♥ Plan a hotel getaway.
- ♥ Have a quickie for lunch.
- ♥ Buy his and her lingerie.
- ♥ Serve her breakfast in bed.
- ♥ Role play.
- ♥ Make love in the car (Be discrete of course).
- ♥ Talk dirty to each other on a phone call.
- ♥ Take a walk on the beach.
- ♥ Hold her all night without making love.
- ♥ Send a love letter.
- ♥ Take an unplanned trip out of town.
- ♥ Make love in your own backyard.
- ♥ Take a balloon bath.

Note: Think of a good one yourself....

Chapter 16

=========

SINGLE AND FREE

Single individuals need to understand more about marriage than what they have heard or seen in other relationships. Understand that their marriage will be like no other marriage; not like their grandparent's, parents, their friends or even like the movie stars'. They must realize that getting married is no picnic because it involves many forms of challenges.

Marriage is not a walk in the park, but a twenty-four hour, seven days a week occupation. When a person finishes their regular job, they must then work even harder on home administration; a function that offers no rest breaks. The swing-shift of a marriage consists of cooking, cleaning, washing clothes, taking the children to their events, walking the dog, organizing and paying the bills, maintaining vehicles, satisfying the spouse, making ready to settle down, and then tucking in for the night to begin a new day.

Being single is not the end of the world. It's not a sin, nor is it a set back, failure or a defeat. It's just another blessing enjoyed by a person who exercises the power of choice.

A single person shouldn't jump into a marriage just because their friends insist that it's the right thing to do. Even if a party becomes pregnant, they shouldn't leap into such a decision.

An unplanned marriage can be a long, hazardous and bumpy ride. It's unwise to marry based on the mere notion of a person going off to college or to the military. Sometimes a couple marries just to keep from losing puppy love. Remember, a puppy love can end up as a disorientated canine affair.

Many single individuals do not care to listen to older adults who have gone down the road that they plan to travel; they only wish to follow in their bliss.

If a married person admits that they would rather be single and lonely, than married and lonely, it clearly indicates that they have traveled down the road of hard knots. Their admittance shouldn't upset the single, but enlighten them, like eating the meat and spiting out the bones. Young people should take the advice and run with it, because an experienced married couple has been on both sides of the fence.

Couples who are married and lonely should by no means try to detour a single individual from marrying, but encourage them to keep their options open.

A single individual's main problem is not so much being "Single and lonely", but "Single and Horney"; it's a hormonal issue, which has motivated many to make wrong decisions in life. God created us with hormones but it's up to us to keep them under control. A person's hormones can send an individual straight to hell, if that individual allows their impulses to gain control of their body. The most critical issue with hormones is when an older spouse begins to lose the effectiveness that hormones once employed. The real question is; can a person continue a marriage in such condition?

Is sex the main ingredient to the relationship? Is it a wonder, why so many marriages break-up when their sexual behavior reaches an all time low? Let's be logical about this issue, with old age all good things comes to an end! Once again, is sex the main ingredient in a marriage or loyalty?

It is strange that some single people want to get marry, while some married people want to become single again. Single people should be advised that when married couples counsels them not to marry, they are merely conveying that marriage is wonderful, but don't believe all the ballyhoo about it.

The main concern about a marriage is to use caution before walking into it. Make sure that you realize all the repercussions related to the relationship. Be mature and do not plan to marry while at the same moment planning an annulment. If an annulment is already a part of a person's thought process, it is obvious that he or she isn't ready. Marriage is about giving your body, your time, your dreams, thoughts, energy, and everything a person owns to another person. There must be equal contribution, whereas a selfish person will not make a good team player.

A single person needs to acknowledge and remember this one importance; if a person can't live by themselves, then it is likely that they can't live with someone else.

Here is good food for thought, let a single person remain unmarried as long as possible, before committing themselves to a totally different life style. So many people are married and lonely because they miss that once single life of being their own boss. It's like having their own business with no one to report to.

A single person should enjoy life while trusting Jesus with all of their decisions, because only God knows best.

Chapter 17

OPEN MARRIAGE

An open marriage is the consent of a husband and wife in agreement to basically do their own thing, without hurting the other person's feelings. Even though they're married, they live as if they're single. They should just come to the agreement to separate rather than sully their marriage vows if they wish to share their bodies with other couples, having threesomes, foursomes, and just plain orgies!

An open marriage is not just limited to sexuality; it involves the activity of romantic communications, secret outside financial help, and exploring wild fantasies and exotic dreams with the same sex and/or opposite sex.

An open marriage is exactly what it says. It's open for anyone to do as they please. Naturally if anything is left open it leaves room for anyone to enter, and do as they please. If a person leaves their home with the doors wide open, they shouldn't be alarmed to find their home in disarray upon returning. This is a perfect picture of an open marriage.

Open marriages are really another way of becoming single with a marriage certificate. If singleness is what a person desires, then why marry. The bible says: "There's nothing new under the sun". An open marriage was a part of Abram and Sarai beginning, though some individuals believe it's something new and popular. They believe that if good old Hollywood can do it, then it must be a part of God's plan. Listen, Hollywood doesn't rule God, but God rules Hollywood! His word doesn't change (cf. Mal. 3:6; Matt. 24:35-36; Heb. 13:8).

Genesis 16

1 Now Sarai, Abram's wife, bare him no children: and she had a handmaid, an Egyptian, whose name was Hagar.

2 And Sarai said unto Abram, Behold now, Jehovah hath restrained me from bearing; go in, I pray thee, unto my handmaid; it may be that I shall obtain children by her. And Abram hearkened to the voice of Sarai.

3 And Sarai, Abram's wife, took Hagar the Egyptian, her handmaid, after Abram had dwelt ten years in the land of Canaan, and gave her to Abram her husband to be his wife.

4 And he went in unto Hagar, and she conceived: and when she saw that she had conceived, her mistress was despised in her eyes.

5 And Sarai said unto Abram, My wrong be upon thee: I gave my handmaid into they bosom; and when she saw that she had conceived, I was despised in her eyes: Jehovah judge between me and thee.

6 But Abram said unto Sarai, Behold, thy maid is in thy hand; do to her that which is good in thine eyes. And Sarai dealt hardly with her, and she fled from her face.

7 And the angel of Jehovah found her by a fountain of water in the wilderness, by the fountain in the way to Shur.

8 And he said, Hagar, Sarai's handmaid, whence camest thou? and whither goest thou? And she said, I am fleeing from the face of my mistress Sarai.

9 And the angel of Jehovah said unto her, Return to thy mistress, and submit thyself under her hands.

10 And the angel of Jehovah said unto her, I will greatly multiply thy seed, that it shall not be numbered for multitude.

11 And the angel of Jehovah said unto her, Behold, thou art with child, and shalt bear a son; and thou shalt call his name Ishmael, because Jehovah hath heard thy affliction.

12 And he shall be as a wild ass among men; his hand shall be against every man, and every man's hand against him; and he shall dwell over against all his brethren.

13 And she called the name of Jehovah that spake unto her, Thou art a God that seeth: for she said, Have I even here looked after him that seeth me?

14 Wherefore the well was called Beer-lahai-roi; behold, it is between Kadesh and Bered.

15 And Hagar bare Abram a son: and Abram called the name of his son, whom Hagar bare, Ishmael.

16 And Abram was fourscore and six years old, when Hagar bare Ishmael to Abram.

As one look at the life of Abram and Sarai, they'll see that an open marriage can and will back fire in the long run, causing much danger and future fatalities. Sarai gave Abram the green light to a situation she felt she could handle, but discovered later that such decision nearly destroyed a relationship with Abram and God. It is prudent to understand that an open marriage is a disaster from the start; a diabolic path where wise men never travel tread.

Most people, who live in an open marriage, are really living a lie. They are married, lonely and trying to find an alternative to fix their situation. It will only get worse until Jesus steps in.

A person can not go into an open marriage with a contract, or an agreement. No individual can tame or control their own emotions in an ungodly affair, which is already designed for failure. Can one imagine telling their spouse to observe these rules of engagement in an open marriage? (Just to name a few).

RULES OF ENGAGEMENT

- Don't fall in love
- No secret dating
- No secret calls
- Only one partner per week
- We will not allow our marriage to suffer
- We will stay faithful to each other

- We will never tell family members or children about our life style
- We will control our feelings
- We will not compare lovers or dates
- We will not take money or gifts
- We will not endanger our relationship with one another

After looking at some of the rules of engagement for open marriages, it looks like a distressed couple trying to nurse a weakened marriage over a dead end road going nowhere. It's like trying to take an enhancement to boost up something that's beyond repair, or a body part that's non-salvageable.

Open marriage is so strong in today's society that a person doesn't have to go far habit, lust or sin.

I am/ We are a:

	Man
	Woman
	Couple (man and woman)
	Couple (two women)
	Couple (two men)
	Straight man
	Straight woman
	Bi couples
	Gay couples
	Lesbian couples
	Group
	Young adult

	Interesting in meeting: a Man a Woman a Couple (man and woman) a Group a Homosexual a Lesbian
	For: Erotic Fantasies Friendships Threesomes Wild sex Group sex (7 or more) Bondage & Discipline Miscellaneous Fetishes Casual sex Exhibition & Voyeurism Soft Swapping One night stand Hard Swapping

An open marriage is like going to a fast food restaurant and ordering what ever is on the menu. This can be quite dangerous to those who are diabetics or food allergies.

Participants in open marriages may prefer different kinds of extramarital relationships. Those who prefer adulterous relationships are surely emotionally involved in a polygamous style of practice. Those same victims fall under the same description "Married and lonely". They all share common issues: the lack of social acceptance, the need to maintain the relationship as an orgy couple, and the need to perpetuate and manage jealous rivalries.

Chapter 18

=========

SOUL TIES

Soul ties come to pass when one's soul, intellect, body, spirit, emotions, impulses and feelings are tied up with someone else's. It's precisely as it says, a person's life is caught-up into another's life with sex. I'm not going to use the word making love in this description, because sex and making love are different.

Individuals can be so entangled with each other until a relationship becomes enslavement. The bible says: "The two shall become one flesh". In the eyes of God, the two really equal one whole thing; never fifty-fifty. Only an act of transgression can make the situation grow worse.

The joining of "Soul ties" can also play a positive role by preventing a married couple from separating; just like tying a shoe knot. When a person's mental state is interwoven with the spirit of another person, they have a united cohesion if the two are married. On the other hand, "Soul's ties" can ruin a marriage when a spouse becomes "Married and lonely", and chooses to go outside the marriage to look for happiness. The human race is now living in a period when sex is an all-time issue. The bible talks about fornication and adultery. The schools, television, computers, radios and all other forms of communication make sex an inescapable issue. But there is one thing those sources are not stressing, and that is the sin and heartache behind sex, if not practiced in a Godly way, or "Guided by God's manual".

When a person has sex with another person they will automatically become one flesh, and actually take on the character of the other. That is why some married couples begin to favor each other in appearance. When a person allows another into their marriage and express their deepest affections, it can become quite difficult to shake it off, or let go so easily! Even when a person volunteers to let another go, it may still be quite effortful to completely forget that individual. For example, an old song may bring back some wonderful memories, which may influence a person to renew the relationship, even when they thought it was all over. Sometimes it's the old perfume or cologne, a car similar to the one they use to drive, a smile, someone's walk or talk which seems to bring it all right back.

Some "Soul ties" are so effective that just by hearing a person's voice, are seeing their face, every now and then will make a person's cloudy days sunny; "Soul ties" will have a person living a lie! It will destroy a person's home, church, job, friendships, and everything that's connected to their current life and the pursuit of happiness. The sad thing about some "Soul ties" is that they can only end through death, because someone refuses to let the past be the past.

Many of us are reminded of an old saying: "If you lay with dogs, you will wake up with flees!"

Proverb 5: 15-23

5:15 Drink waters out of thine own cistern, and running waters out of thine own well.

5:16 Should thy fountains be dispersed abroad, and rivers of waters in the streets?

5:17 Let them be only thine own, and not strangers' with thee.

5:18 Let thy fountain be blessed: and rejoice with the wife of thy youth.

5:19 Let her be as the loving hind and pleasant roe; let her breasts satisfy thee at all times; and be thou ravished always with her love.

5:20 And why wilt thou, my son, be ravished with a strange woman, and embrace the bosom of a stranger?

Married and Lonely

5:21 For the ways of man are before the eyes of the LORD, and he pondereth all his goings.

5:22 His own iniquities shall take the wicked himself, and he shall be holden with the cords of his sins.

5:23 He shall die without instruction; and in the greatness of his folly he shall go astray.

People need to know that marriage and Salvation are totally different. Most people that are married are not in the church for some strange reason. But God's principle on marriage is for the saved as well as the unsaved.

God ordained the marriage and the sexual intimacy of husband and wife at the very beginning. However, Satan has taken what God has fashioned and attempted to pervert it, by inventing a counterfeit of the original blue print. In this generation with the question "If it feels good, do it?," Satan has convinced us that sexual relations outside a marriage is perfectly common, and shouldn't be frowned upon. He lectures them, "Everybody in the world is doing it," but he doesn't inform them of the consequences of such actions. Some of those consequences are unwanted pregnancies and sexual diseases, but these are other evidence which a person can only see with spiritual eyes. There are other consequences that will be reaped, that can't be observed with the natural eye. It's the spiritual war that our soul is losing. That's why married couples should keep their amusement in their own bedroom, never giving the devil an ounce of victory.

There is one essential that every couple needs to know, and that is; there is no such thing as a one night stand! Yes, that person's body may be many miles away, but the "Soul ties" that were made in minutes or an hour will follow them for the rest of their life.

1 Corinthians 6-15-20

6:15 Know ye not that your bodies are the members of Christ? shall I then take the members of Christ, and make them the members of an harlot? God forbid.

6:16 What? know ye not that he which is joined to an harlot is one body? for two, saith he, shall be one flesh.

6:17 But he that is joined unto the Lord is one spirit.

6:18 Flee fornication. Every sin that a man doeth is without the body; but he that committeth fornication sinneth against his own body.

6:19 What? Know ye not that your body is the temple of the Holy Ghost which is in you, which ye have of God, and ye are not your own?

6:20 For ye are bought with a price: therefore glorify God in your body, and in your spirit, which are God's.

How many souls have been chained to a person's temple, besides God and his or her spouse?

Soul ties with one's husband/wife - Genesis 2:24 "Therefore a man shall leave his father and his mother and shall become united and cleave to his wife, and they shall become one flesh."

Many people are in a state of denial in their relationship. They've had a rocky marriage which ended with divorce, which lead to an even greater problem; After meeting a new interest they could never completely leave their former spouse. The "Soul ties" were so solid until they couldn't let go, finding themselves free of many things in life, but could never shake that first love. The person found that they were only fooling themselves, believing that their feelings would one day change, but unfortunately the "Soul ties" could never be broken.

Soul ties are adultery and fornication - Genesis 34:2,3 "And when Shechem son of Hamor the Hivite, prince of the country, saw her, he seized her, lay with her, and humbled, defiled, and disgraced her. But his soul longed for and clung to Dinah daughter of Jacob, and he loved the girl and spoke comfortingly to her young heart's wishes". This is just one reason to teach your children not to have sex before marriage. Not only is it sin but you form an ungodly soul tie with that person. "Soul ties" with the world-Joshua 23:13 "Know with certainty

that the Lord your God will not continue to drive out these nations from before you; but they shall be a snares and traps unto you, and a scourges in your sides and thorns in your eyes, until you perish from off this land which the Lord your God has given you".

A person can form an ungodly "Soul ties" with anyone or thing. Here are some "Soul ties" that need to be broken in the name of Jesus! If a friend or person could control another to do wrong, then there is an ungodly "Soul tie" - mothers with daughters, fathers with sons, pastors with the congregation, bosses and employees with each other, just to name a few. Having control is one of the key evidence that an ungodly "Soul tie" has been formed. Sometimes a person is unable to see the control of the ungodly "Soul tie". Hindsight is common among us all and this is why a lot of individuals try to break ungodly "Soul ties" with others. Now if there wasn't an ungodly "Soul tie", then a person would have only wasted a little breath. But if there was, then it's just a matter of time before destruction will set in.

Remember ungodly "Soul ties" can be formed no matter how much you love the Lord and worship Him. A person must break ungodly "Soul ties" in Jesus' name. It is very simple and easy to break these ungodly "Soul ties" based upon one's unconditional surrender to God...

> Prayer for "Soul ties": "Lord in the name of Jesus forgive me for all of the unhealthy choices I've made in my life that has formed a "Soul ties". In Jesus' name I will destroy all ungodly "Soul ties" that I have with people, places and things, such as my grandparents, mother, father, brothers, sisters, aunts, uncles, sons, daughters, pastors, other Christians, churches, movie stars, singers, evangelists, my boss, my employees, my doctor, pet, etc". This list can go on and on as the Lord gives a person discernment, which will break each ungodly "Soul tie" in the name of Jesus! In Jesus' name a person

can command all demons of ungodly "Soul ties" to leave his spirit. He can command demonic forces of people, places and things to evacuate the premises. A God fearing person may have to deal with this form of praying throughout their lives in order to rid themselves of all demonic and ungodly "Soul ties". He or she may also have to get rid of every article such as pictures, movies, phone number, cloth or any type of souvenirs that may draw them back into the influence of destruction.

CONCLUSION

After reading this book, I hope it will encourage and help all who thirst for the nourishment of truth.

Married and Lonely is a deep subject which few wish to deal with, because of its taboo. Some people that are married and lonely are living in self-denial. As a nation and a people we don't know who we are, often seeing everyone else's problem except for our own. In a marriage our children can tell us more about us than what we give them credit for. Our children can clearly distinguish the difference between a real and a fake smile. Most married and lonely couples feel like there's no help nor hope for their situation. First of all, all situations are different and must be handled accordingly. In a marriage two separates or a half can never make a whole, but two wholes can consummate an absolute. The marriage must operate on all cylinders, if not, the marriage will begin to knock and miss like a slipping car engine. It is necessary for us to repair the broken box of marriage which is love, communication, sex and finance, if one wishes to achieve the harmony and happiness that marriage offers.

The first approach to repair a shaky marriage is to work on reconciling the differences with patience. Wait on God to see if the fire can be put back. If such approach doesn't work then a person should seek professional counseling, and not just someone with an on-line certificate, but a true Christian with a degree. One of the best places to begin is with one's Pastor. Divorce may not be the answer and only the individuals will know when it's time to run. Just imagine, a short separation might work until the couple gets back on track. In order to put the marriage back on track a couple must know what type of abuse the marriage may be facing. Is it mental, verbal, emotional or physical? All of these abuses will kill a marriage in one way or another. Only a spouse realizes what chapter of a book their life exist in. They should never allow anyone else to close the chapter of their lives together, which has yet to be completed. The chapter becomes closed only when a couple themselves chooses to close it.

When both parties have tried everything to fix their marriage, and all has failed, ending with divorce doesn't mean that all hope has vanished. It doesn't mean that a divorce is the end of the road, since a divorce can enable a couple to go through a different type of extended healing period. Some people are just a little slower to heal than others. Have you ever had a wound that healed well on the outside, but was still tender under the skin? Some people have to go through a similar process following a divorce before healing. Experiencing a life after a divorce could well bring a great benefit. While divorce can be a painful stage of life; Great joy can very much re-occur with new activities as outings, movies, vacations, new associates, along with a renewed approach in serving the Lord. Let's face it; going through a divorce is not the end of the world, because one person's junk can be another person's treasure.

Remember, Jesus is always there for us. A person can hear the voice Jesus within saying, "I will always be with you", even while going through their "Married and lonely" period. When a person becomes distressed, they can hear Jesus saying, "I Am here". Before a person even met their spouse, Jesus was with them! Once again enjoy life, because it's a gift and too short to waste. Now, one thing a person doesn't want to do, is to jump into another marriage in order to heal a painful hurt or to fill the void left by a previous situation.

Once a person has acknowledged that they are truly "Married and lonely", this book can give them the insight to see the signs, that a marriage will only become what a couple makes of it". A marriage will work, if a person will work with it!

A Woman's Desires

A woman's desires are different from man's desire. What a woman wants is:

- Quality time with her husband
- A listening ear
- Romance
- Affection
- To feel loved
- To feel wanted
- To cuddle
- To be complimented
- Walks in the park
- To go for rides in the car
- To watch television together
- A man that's not afraid of work
- A Real Man

A Man Desires

Men desires are different from what women desire. What a man wants is:

- Support from his wife
- Peace of mind
- A wife that can take care of the home
- A clean wife
- A smart wife
- A trusting wife
- A wife that loves God

HOW WELL DO YOU KNOW YOUR SPOUSE?

1. Spouse's favorite gift.
2. Spouse's nickname for the bed room.
3. Spouse's favorite bible story.
4. Spouse's birth city.
5. Spouse's favorite NBA team.

Married and Lonely

6. The most times you and spouse make love in one week.
7. Household chore your spouse dislikes most.
8. If money was no object the first thing your spouse would do.
9. Spouse's favorite bible verse.
10. Spouse's favorite bible character.
11. Spouse's favorite NFL team.
12. Spouse's favorite color.
13. Spouse's height.
14. Spouse's weight.
15. Spouse's birth mark.
16. Spouse's favorite dress/suit.
17. Spouse's favorite game show.
18. Spouse's sexiest night cloth.
19. Spouse's pet peeve.
20. Spouse's favorite room in the house.
21. Spouse's favorite Aunt.
22. Spouse's favorite Uncle.
23. Most sensitive part of spouse's body.
24. Spouse's favorite State.
25. Spouse's favorite sex position.
26. Spouse's least favorite sex position.
27. Spouse's shoe size.
28. Spouse's favorite animal.
29. Spouse's High School.
30. Spouse's favorite meal.
31. Spouse's favorite restaurant.
32. Spouse's favorite sport.
33. Spouse's favorite soap opera.
34. Spouse's favorite news station.
35. Spouse's favorite actor.
36. Spouse's favorite actress.
37. Spouse's favorite cartoon.
38. Spouse's favorite truck.
39. Spouse's favorite car.
40. Spouse's favorite SUV or ATV.
41. Spouse's favorite day of the week.
42. Spouse's favorite Month of the year.

43. Spouse's favorite Holiday.
44. Spouse's suit size.
45. Spouse's favorite book.
46. Spouse's favorite magazine.
47. Spouse's favorite Season of the year.
48. Spouse's Best Friend.
49. Spouse's worst habit.
50. Spouse's favorite deodorant.
51. Spouse's favorite soap.
52. Spouse's favorite tooth paste.
53. Spouse's worst argument.
54. Spouse's favorite Supermarket.
55. Spouse's favorite R&B song.
56. Spouse's favorite Country song.
57. Spouse's favorite Gospel artist.
58. Spouse's favorite Rapper.
59. Spouse's favorite Singer.
60. Spouse's favorite subject in school.
61. Spouse's least favorite subject in school.
62. Spouse's first gift from you.
63. Spouse's most use word.
64. Spouse's favorite Movie.
65. Spouse's most embarrassing moment.
66. Spouse's favorite Board Game.
67. Spouse's favorite vacation spot.
68. Spouse's favorite Niece.
69. Spouse's favorite Nephew.
70. Spouse's most desirable time for sex.
71. Spouse's favorite style of kissing.
72. Spouse's most memorable sex location.
73. Spouse's most daring sex location.
74. Spouse's favorite ice cream.
75. Spouse's favorite tree.
76. Spouse's favorite bird.
77. Spouse's favorite flower.
78. Spouse's favorite plant.
79. Spouse's favored hand.

80. Spouse's favorite desert.
81. Spouse's favorite pair of jeans.
82. Spouse's favorite cereal.
83. Spouse's favorite soda.
84. Spouse's favorite piece of jewelry.
85. Spouse's greatest fear.
86. Spouse's greatest strength.
87. Spouse's greatest weakness.
88. Spouse's retirement plan.
89. Spouse's favorite fruit.
90. Spouse's favorite horror movie.
91. Most times Spouse had sex in one day.
92. Spouse most favorite sexual turn-on.
93. Spouse's most favored Relative.
94. Spouse's most favored Author.
95. Spouse's favorite hobby.
96. Spouse's favorite hat.
97. Spouse's favorite candy bar.
98. Spouse's favorite Reality Show.
99. Spouse's most memorable date.
100. Spouse's most favored picture.

ASSESSMENT SCALE

0-25: Low. (Married and lonely.)

26-75: AVERAGE. (Not bad at all.)

76-100: MARRIAGE FITNESS CHAMPION.
(Great job, keep up the good work!)

How well do you know your spouse?

Answer sheet:

1.
2.
3.
4.
5.
6.
7.
8.
9.
10.
11.
12.
13.
14.
15.
16.
17.
18.
19.
20.
21.
22.
23.
24.
25.
26.
27.
28.
29.
30.
31.
32.
33.

34.
35.
36.
37.
38.
39.
40.
41.
42.
43.
44.
45.
46.
47.
48.
49.
50.
51.
52.
53.
54.
55.
56.
57.
58.
59.
60.
61.
62.
63.
64.
65.
66.
67.
68.
69.
70.

71.
72.
73.
74.
75.
76.
77.
78.
79.
80.
81.
82.
83.
84.
85.
86.
87.
88.
89.
90.
91.
92.
93.
94.
95.
96.
97.
98.
99.
100.

Food for thought

What will it take for someone to steal your spouse? Husband and wife, too many rejections in a marriage will eventually cause a spouse to not want to participate in future love making and seek after others.

Stop crying, complaining, stressing out, getting vindictive, wanting to commit suicide when a spouse walk out or leave you for no reason. Celebrate and move on with your life.

Never divorce and jump quickly into another relationship.

Seize every moment with your spouse. Tomorrow is not promised.

Marriage today needs a contract with the signing of one's marriage certificate to keep a spouse from losing everything: For example, if a spouse leaves or divorce another spouse for no apparent reason, or just because that spouse wants a new spouse. The contract is to pay that spouse $50,000 for psychological pain and suffering.

- Never give up on you, Due to a failed marriage.
- A successful marriage has to run in order, to run correct.
- Marriage should be like expensive wine, it gets better with time.
- Study your spouse, and read yourself.
- An old saying, one man's junk is another mans treasures, just because you don't value your spouse. It does not mean that nobody else will.
- Close the chapters on all pass relationship.

MARRIED AND LONELY JOURNAL

Date:
Time:
My thoughts of the day:

MARRIED AND LONELY JOURNAL

Date:
Time:
My thoughts of the day:

MARRIED AND LONELY JOURNAL

Date:
Time:
My thoughts of the day:

MARRIED AND LONELY JOURNAL

Date:
Time:
My thoughts of the day:

MARRIED AND LONELY JOURNAL

Date:
Time:
My thoughts of the day:

MARRIED AND LONELY JOURNAL

Date:
Time:
My thoughts of the day:

MARRIED AND LONELY JOURNAL

Date:
Time:
My thoughts of the day:

MARRIED AND LONELY JOURNAL

Date:
Time:
My thoughts of the day:

MARRIED AND LONELY JOURNAL

Date:
Time:
My thoughts of the day:

MARRIED AND LONELY JOURNAL

Date:
Time:
My thoughts of the day:

MARRIED AND LONELY JOURNAL

Date:
Time:
My thoughts of the day:

MARRIED AND LONELY JOURNAL

Date:
Time:
My thoughts of the day:

MARRIED AND LONELY JOURNAL

Date:
Time:
My thoughts of the day:

MARRIED AND LONELY JOURNAL

Date:
Time:
My thoughts of the day:

MARRIED AND LONELY JOURNAL

Date:
Time:
My thoughts of the day:

MARRIED AND LONELY JOURNAL

Date:
Time:
My thoughts of the day:

MARRIED AND LONELY JOURNAL

Date:
Time:
My thoughts of the day:

MARRIED AND LONELY JOURNAL

Date:
Time:
My thoughts of the day:

MARRIED AND LONELY JOURNAL

Date:
Time:
My thoughts of the day:

MARRIED AND LONELY JOURNAL

Date:
Time:
My thoughts of the day:

MARRIED AND LONELY JOURNAL

Date:
Time:
My thoughts of the day:

MARRIED AND LONELY JOURNAL

Date:
Time:
My thoughts of the day:

MARRIED AND LONELY JOURNAL

Date:
Time:
My thoughts of the day:

MARRIED AND LONELY JOURNAL

Date:
Time:
My thoughts of the day:

MARRIED AND LONELY JOURNAL

Date:
Time:
My thoughts of the day:

MARRIED AND LONELY JOURNAL

Date:
Time:
My thoughts of the day:

MARRIED AND LONELY JOURNAL

Date:
Time:
My thoughts of the day:

MARRIED AND LONELY JOURNAL

Date:
Time:
My thoughts of the day:

MARRIED AND LONELY JOURNAL

Date:
Time:
My thoughts of the day:

MARRIED AND LONELY JOURNAL

Date:
Time:
My thoughts of the day:

MARRIED AND LONELY JOURNAL

Date:
Time:
My thoughts of the day:

Printed in the United States
212560BV00001B/180/P